TOFU HOLLANDAISE SAUCE

makes 1½ cups

½ cup soft tofu
2 tablespoons lemon juice
¼ teaspoon salt
Pinch of cayenne
½ to ⅔ cup melted butter

Combine the tofu, lemon juice, salt, and cayenne in a blender jar. Have the heated butter ready. Blend the tofu mixture at low speed and increase to the highest speed. Add the butter by droplets at first, and then increase to a steady stream.

The sauce should be served immediately, without reheating. There is seldom a failure when using tofu instead of eggs. If there should be some separation of fat, reblend but do not heat.

JUEL ANDERSEN'S TOFU KITCHEN

Juel Andersen
Illustrations by
Juel Andersen

BANTAM BOOKS
TORONTO · NEW YORK · LONDON · SYDNEY

JUEL ANDERSEN'S TOFU KITCHEN
A Bantam Book / January 1982

ISBN 0-553-20424-6

Published simultaneously in the United States and Canada

Bantam Books are published by Bantam Books, Inc. Its trademark,
consisting of the words "Bantam Books" and the portrayal of a
rooster, is Registered in U.S. Patent and Trademark Office and in
other countries. Marca Registrada. Bantam Books, Inc., 666 Fifth
Avenue, New York, New York 10103.

PRINTED IN THE UNITED STATES OF AMERICA

0 9 8 7 6 5 4 3 2 1

To John, to Tia, and to Tofu

CONTENTS

INTRODUCTION

TOFU ???

When I sit down to a dinner of a perfectly broiled filet mignon, French fried potatoes, warm, crisp bread, and a Caesar salad, with cheese pie for dessert, I do not think about all the marvelous protein I am about to consume.

I do not think about how this meal is going to build healthy muscle tissue and supply me with nutrients that my body is unable to make for itself. I proceed to eat this very expensive, high prestige meal, and I enjoy every bite because it tastes good and I like it.

When I sit down to a dinner of crabmeat crepes, served with hollandaise sauce, a warm whole-grain roll, a green salad with blue cheese dressing, with New York cheesecake for dessert, I do not think about all the marvelous protein I am about to eat either. No, I am going to eat this delicious, very inexpensive, seemingly rich food and enjoy every bite, because it tastes good and I like it, too.

I like both of these dinners, but perhaps I prefer the second one because I feel good about what I am eating. I know that I am doing something special for myself. I have cut out most of the cholesterol from these excessively rich foods. I have actually increased the amount of high-quality protein I have eaten. I have reduced the calories to a fraction of what they could have been, and I have spent so little money that I can actually afford to buy filet mignon. I did it by using tofu in each and every dish.

Maybe you haven't heard much about tofu yet. The name is more unfamiliar than the food. Most people recognize it when they are told that it is the white cubes found in soups in Chinese restaurants. It is also known as bean curd or soybean curd or soy cheese. The Japanese call it "tofu" (toe-Fu) and the Chinese call it "doufu" (Doe-FU).

I call it tofu and I also call it "marvelous." I use it every day and in many ways. It has become so much a part of my cooking, that I would as soon be out of flour or sugar as be out of tofu. I almost said eggs, butter, and milk, but now that I cook with tofu, being out of them is not so serious.

I use tofu in dishes for every meal of the day and for in-between snacks too. I use it straight from the package as a separate food, and I use it in many more ways as an ingredient, in sauces and salad dressings and dips, in spreads and fillings, in pies and puddings, in cakes and cookies, and . . . but why go on, it is all here in this book.

I have found tofu to be *my* miracle food. Five years of using it has not lessened my enthusiasm. I want to share my excitement with you and help you to start on this new adventure in cooking and eating.

So, please, for the while it takes to get acquainted, put away your wok and your prejudices and just think of tofu as a newly invented ingredient that has magical powers to be explored. Put on your apron, and join me in the kitchen.

1

TOFU IS . . .

Tofu, made from soybeans, looks like a soft, white cheese. It is bland, having little taste of its own, but it will take on the flavor of whatever it is cooked with. This lack of a strong character makes tofu very versatile.

Made from soy milk in much the same way that cottage cheese is made from cow's milk, tofu is comparable to fresh milk products such as yogurt, cottage cheese, cream cheese, and ricotta, and has about the same amount of protein, fat, and carbohydrates as these dairy products. Tofu can be used in all the ways milk products can be used—and in many more ways, too.

Tofu is also comparable to the egg. Some say that eggs are nature's most nearly perfect food. It certainly has nature's most nearly perfect package. But tofu can do *almost* everything an egg can do and do it without any cholesterol at all.

Tofu is different from these products in as many ways as it is similar. Comparing it to them just gives us a starting place.

TELL ME MORE . . .

In spite of its simple appearance and bland taste, tofu is a gem among foods. It is high in protein and low in calories; it is low in saturated fat and cholesterol-free; and it is easily digested by the most delicate constitution. Tofu is also rich in vitamins and minerals.

Unlike cattle, who make protein from grass, we must eat the protein we need to replenish our bodies. We are in the habit of getting this protein from animal foods such as meat, fish, poultry, eggs, and cow's milk products. We tend not to know much about vegetable sources of protein, although everything we eat has some protein, even lettuce.

Grains and seeds are high in protein. Peas and beans are even higher; but the prince of vegetable protein is the soybean.

The protein in the tofu made from soybeans is entirely comparable to that in beef or chicken or any animal food. If it is deficient, so is beef. To bring the protein up in both of them, it is wise and necessary to eat another food along with beef or tofu to increase the amount of protein that we can use. One of these foods is wheat.

It is interesting that by custom, we eat bread with beef. The protein in the wheat that the bread is made from complements the protein in the beef, making more of it available to our bodies. This way of eating is very natural to Americans and Westerners generally. Eating corn, beans, and rice is natural to many other nationalities. Beef and wheat make a complete protein; corn, beans and rice in combination make a complete protein.

If tofu is eaten with wheat bread, rice, and certain seeds, the amount of protein available to us can be increased by as much as 40 percent. It is wise to complement* soy protein with these foods, either at the same meal or at some time during the same day. It is not necessary to make a cult of this. It is something to keep in mind when eating tofu and when eating meat. You might just as well get all the protein that is coming to you.

Most high protein foods are also high in calories. Tofu has the lowest fat to protein ratio of any such food. Choice quality porterhouse steak is as much as 42 percent fat; indeed, it is the fat marbling that makes it tender. Cooked chicken is about 12 percent fat; chicken eggs are 11.5 percent fat. These are all high cholesterol foods; tofu is 4 percent fat and has no cholesterol at all.

That tofu is cholesterol-free is of immense value, especially to people who have high cholesterol levels and an insatiable love of rich foods. The ways in which tofu can

* For an explanation of "protein complementarity" see Appendix 1.

be used instead of high-fat dairy foods are almost limit-less, as you will soon see.

Tofu is a precooked protein food. When you buy it or make it yourself, it needs no further cooking. Since it is a protein extract from the soybean, it contains very little of the substances that many people find hard to digest in fatty meats and whole beans.

For people on allergy diets or fat-restricted diets or weight loss diets or diets of any kind, tofu has a special appeal. It can be used instead of eggs, cheese, milk, and meat in an array of delicious foods that you will not be able to believe until you have tried them.

A VERY BRIEF HISTORICAL NOTE

No one knows quite when the Chinese invented "doufu," but it was written about as early as the second century B.C. It is thought that the soybean was taken to Japan by Buddhist missionaries from Korea and China sometime between the third and the eighth centuries of our Christian era. The first mention of the soybean in Japanese writings appeared in 712 A.D., and by then it is known that soybean foods were important in the Japanese diet.*

It is perhaps an accident of fate and an injustice to the Chinese that the name "tofu," which is the Japanese equivalent of their "doufu," should have become our accepted name. But the name is incidental; what is really important to know is that the peoples of the Orient have been using the soybean and eating tofu for centuries, probably longer than 2,000 years.

It is surprising that tofu took so long to cross the Pacific, but now that it has arrived its fame is spreading rapidly.

*Shurtleff, William and Aoyagi, Akiko; The Book of Tofu; Ballantine Books, New York, N. Y. 1979. pp. 58–63

MORE ABOUT TOFU

WHERE CAN I GET TOFU?

Tofu is available in almost every community these days. If it is not in the supermarket, it will certainly be found in "natural" or "health" food stores. It usually comes in plastic tubs that contain a block or slices of tofu weighing anywhere from 10 ounces to 22 ounces.

There are two types of tofu widely available: the softer Japanese kind and the firm Chinese kind. There are other kinds, too. One is "kinogoshi" or "silken" tofu, which is very smooth and light, but has limited uses.

The Japanese kind, I call soft tofu. It has a higher water content than the Chinese type, which I call firm tofu. The Chinese style is not as smooth as the Japanese.

If you are unable to buy tofu, you can make it yourself in your own kitchen. It is not difficult. I prove that by making it myself, once or twice a week. It is easier to make than bread, takes less time and requires very little special equipment.

It is not necessary to buy two kinds of tofu. If the Japanese variety is available, you can press the water out in a very simple procedure and make it as firm as you want (see page 7 for instructions). I make only *one* kind of tofu, the soft kind, and it serves me for all of tofu's many uses.

IS TOFU EXPENSIVE?

Tofu is quite cheap compared to other forms of high-protein food. It will cost about half as much as the cheapest hamburger and be far cheaper than any other kind of meat. This should be enough to convince almost anyone to try tofu. But the real benefit is that you can make so many high-protein treats from tofu—pies and cakes and shakes and sauces an dips and salad dressings—things you can't make at all from hamburger or lamb chops.

If you learn to make your own tofu, it will cost just pennies a pound. Tofu is cheap, but soybeans are cheaper. One pound of soybeans will yield between 2½ and

3½ pounds of tofu and about 2½ pounds of solids called "okara." On the way to making tofu, you will make soy milk that can be used instead of cow's milk for any use. One pound of soybeans will make about 7 quarts of a non-cholesterol milk that is equivalent to the high-priced product in almost every respect.*

IS TOFU PURE?

We are very concerned these days about the purity of the foods we eat. There are so many tales of adulterants and additives that we have become suspicious of_everything. Tofu is certainly one of the purest foods to be found. Thus far there are no additives in commercial tofu, other than the necessary natural solidifiers or curdling agents that are used.

Not only is nothing added to tofu, but being a vegetable product it has the least possible amount of environmental contaminants. Soybeans may be sprayed while they are growing, and may be fed with artificial fertilizers, but animals feed on these same contaminants. In the case of beef, for example, it takes about 22 pounds of high-grade, high-protein, highly sprayed, and highly fertilized feed to produce *one pound of beef*.

Whatever form of tofu you use, the really crucial thing to know is whether it is *fresh* or *old*. Tofu should be treated as a dairy product, with identical standards for freshness. You would be quite annoyed to open a container of sour cream or cottage cheese to find it smelling like rotten eggs or having an unpleasant flavor. If you have bought tofu and found it sour, it is because it is *old*. If it smells like rotten eggs it is *old*. If it is a bit slimy, it is more than just old—it is *ancient*.

Many grocers think it should be kept in the produce case with the carrots, spinach, and bean sprouts. Tofu does not belong there, it belongs in a refrigerated case. It should be treated exactly as milk and cottage cheese, and

*Soy milk is deficient in calcium. It is easy to supplement this with a variety of easily obtained and inexpensive preparations. See Appendix 1 for nutritional information.

it should be dated so that the customer can know if it is fresh or not.

Chinese and Japanese people buy tofu every day and insist that it be fresh. If it is more than a day old, it is deep fried, dried, or frozen.

It may be that in the future someone will make a junk food of tofu, but it hasn't happened yet. If it should happen—as it has happened with yogurt—you can avoid all the problems by making your own tofu and reaping the additional reward of being virtuous. If you are a real purist, you can even grow your own soybeans.

USING TOFU . . .

Tofu is the most versatile food I have ever found. It fits into every meal and into snacks and treats as well. It can be used in waffles and pancakes for breakfast; in sandwiches and salads and salad dressings for lunch; in casseroles and hearty main dishes for dinner, and in deliciously wicked desserts.

Before discussing cooking with tofu, there is more you should know about its nature. I am going to assume that in the "getting familiar" stage you will be buying tofu. You may soon wish to become a tofu-maker, and that is my best hope for you. But until then, taking first things first, let me tell you what to do with tofu when you bring it home.

HOW SHOULD TOFU BE STORED?

If you buy tofu, or make it yourself, the storage is the same. It must be refrigerated, of course, but it need not be stored in water unless you choose to do so. Most packages of tofu will instruct you to drain the tofu, rinse it, and then add fresh water to cover it. You are also told to change the water daily.

I like to use tofu for different dishes on different days. When it is fresh it is sweet and very light and does best in recipes that take advantage of those features. In the days following, it will lose water and become more solid and firm. Then it can be used for dishes calling for firmer tofu.

Storing tofu under water will help to maintain its bulk. It will not make it stay fresh longer.

HOW LONG WILL IT STAY FRESH?

If you buy tofu from a special tofu shop, or if you make it yourself and you *know* when it was made, it can be used for up to two weeks. If you buy it in a package that is not dated, it may last for about a week.

We have learned to look at the date on dairy product cartons. In many states this dating is controlled by law, and products that pass the "pull date" must not be sold. If sold, the customer must know that she is buying "old" goods.

There are no controls on tofu and it is very possible to buy undated tofu that is spoiled. If the tofu smells bad or tastes sour, I suggest you take it right back to the store-keeper and gently suggest that he ask his supplier to date the tofu so that everyone will know how old it is. Get your money back, too.

I got into a discussion with a produce man who insisted that tofu never spoils. We settled the difference of opinion by opening a sealed (but undated) package. The odor caused several shoppers to look around to see who had committed this indiscretion. The man was very embarrassed and very sheepish. He still believes this one package was an exception—but **he is wrong!**

NOW ABOUT FIRM AND SOFT TOFU . . .

Firm tofu and soft tofu are just about the same. The only difference is in the amount of water contained in the curd. It is easy to make a solid tofu from fresh, soft tofu. You must remove water by pressing out the excess. Here are two easy ways to do this:

If you need mashed firm tofu and you don't care if it retains its shape, put it in a clean dish towel and just twist and squeeze it until it loses the required amount of moisture.

If you wish to slice or cube firm tofu, wrap it in paper towels and press it between two flat surfaces with a weight on top. I usually make what I call a "pressing sandwich" on the kitchen counter. First, I use a pile of newspaper to absorb the water. Then the tofu, wrapped in paper towels or between two layers of toweling. Then another pad of newspaper; then a flat board or plate, and a weight on top to do the job quickly. It takes about 5 to 10 minutes to get nice firm tofu from fresh, soft tofu.

When you know how to press tofu, you need only buy or make one kind. You will be able to vary the water content and, therefore, the firmness, at will.

WHAT CAN BE DONE WITH OLD TOFU?

If you have tofu that is just a bit tainted or old, don't despair. And don't throw it away. You can revive it and you can use it in some very impressive ways.

Parboiling or Steaming Tofu

The first thing you can do to restore the tofu is to parboil or steam it. Cut it in convenient slices or chunks, put it in a saucepan or steamer with about 2 inches of water and bring it to a boil. Reduce the heat and let the tofu simmer or steam for 15 minutes. This will kill the bacteria. The tofu will become light, puffy, and very moist. Use it as you would fresh tofu.

Freezing and Thawing Tofu

If you do not plan to use the tofu you have revived by boiling right away, or if you have some old tofu that is left over because tofu-making day has arrived, just put it in a plastic bag or other container and freeze it. It will wait for you indefinitely.

When you have a good supply of odd chunks, perhaps two or three cups or a couple of large blocks, remove them from the freezer and thaw, either at room temperature for several hours, or in a bowl of warm water.

You will be surprised by this "new" tofu. It will be different in color: a creamy beige. And it will be a different texture; very like a cellulose sponge. But don't be fooled. That strange-looking stuff is the pure gold of foodstuffs—a web of high-quality protein.

Using Thawed Tofu

The first thing you must do with thawed tofu is get the water out of it, and that is done by pressing it just as you would fresh tofu (page 7). Now you have a fairly dry, spongy mass of tofu and you can do any of a number of things with it:

1. Crumble it and use it in spaghetti sauce.
2. Mix it with ground meat as an extender.
3. Combine it with grains, vegetables, nuts or seeds to make vegetarian "meat."
4. Use it instead of firm tofu for tofuburgers.
5. Add it to soups.
6. Marinate the cubes and use in shish kebabs.
7. Cube and deep fry to use as croutons or in Sweet and Sour Tofu, or other dishes.
8. Cube or slice thinly, deep fry, season and use for high-protein snacks.
9. Mash or crumble it and use it for PSP.

What is PSP?

The letters TVP™ stand for Textured Vegetable Protein. This is the trademark of a commercial product made from soy flour. It is extruded, flavored, dried, and colored. When mixed with water it becomes usable as a meat extender and as an ingredient in mock-meat products.

You can make something much better than the commercial TVP™. It is very like ground meat in texture and can be used instead of ground meat—or as an addition to it. It is easy to make and will keep for months, if refrigerated, and for weeks on the pantry shelf. It has been called PSP, which stands for *Processed Soy Protein*, and the *process* involves using the thawed tofu described above.

Making PSP

If you have frozen, thawed, and squeezed the water from tofu, you have done half the job of making PSP. The next step is to crumble or mash it into pieces about the size of corn or rice kernels. I find a pastry fork good for this, or a quick pulse of the blender (do a small amount at a time), or just crumbling it with my fingers.

After crumbling, mix it with a flavoring in these proportions: 2 tablespoons liquid flavor to 1 cup loosely packed crumbled tofu. The flavoring can be soy sauce, bouillon, strong soup stock, fish stock (court bouillon), clam juice or any flavor you like.

Spread the flavored tofu on a cookie sheet and bake in a slow oven, about 250°F. to 275°F., for an hour or more, or until it is dry and brown. Cool on the sheet and store in a tightly closed container, either in the refrigerator or on the shelf. It will keep indefinitely, if refrigerated. Since tofu is 4 percent fat, it will tend to become rancid if stored for a long time without refrigeration.

Using PSP

The most striking characteristic of PSP is the change that takes place in the texture of the tofu after it has been frozen and dried. It will never again be soft, no matter how much water you add to it. It will absorb just so much water and no more. The texture is very like that of ground beef. Indeed, some vegetarian friends refused to eat my spaghetti sauce until I proved to them that I had not used ground meat. Thus, the most logical use for PSP is as a ground meat substitute:

1. PSP instead of ground meat

   1 cup PSP
   ½ to 1 cup very hot water
   2 tablespoons oil (about 15 percent fat)

Mix the PSP with hot water and allow to stand until it absorbs much as it can. Pour off excess water and mix in the fat. Use in meat loaf and meat sauces. Add to tofuburger mix as desired. Use in Chili Con PSP and for Sloppy Joe's. Add to filling recipes.

Note: PSP will not stay together the way raw meat does. Don't forget, it is a fully cooked food.

2. PSP as a snack or in salads

The PSP can be used as a high protein snack. If you would like cubes, slices, or sticks, do not mash the thawed tofu, but cut it into forms and press out the water as described on page 7. Dip the pieces in your choice of flavoring mixture. Bake the forms in a slow oven (250°F. to 275°F.) for an hour or more, or until crisp. This makes excellent food for campers and backpackers. Dry PSP is more than 50 percent protein.*

*Excerpted in part from *The Tofu Cookbook* © 1979 by Cathy Bauer and Juel Andersen. Permission granted by Rodale Press, Inc., Emmaus, PA 18049. Pages 41–43.

2

MAKING TOFU AND SOY MILK
(and Okara, too)

Are you intrigued by the possibilities of this new food? Have you been disappointed by the kind of tofu you have been able to buy? Or maybe you haven't been able to buy it at all, or have found it to be too expensive, in spite of my promises that it is the most economical protein you will find.

You can solve all these problems by making tofu in your own kitchen and, as a bonus, making a very valuable extra product at the same time.

If you still think that tofu is exotic and difficult, it may be because you are not familiar with it. Let me assure you that there is no need to be shy. Tofu is about as exotic as potatoes, bread, or boiled rice. There is no need to bow or invoke spirits; just get yourself a pound of dry soybeans, a small box of ordinary Epsom salts and a water faucet, and you will be in the tofu business for yourself.

ABOUT SOY MILK

The first recipe below is for making soy milk. This is the basis of tofu, just as cow's milk is the basis of cheese. Some people are so stunned to find that they can make delicious, fresh, soy milk themselves that they stop right there and never get to the tofu. Fresh soy milk is very difficult to buy. The unpalatable liquid you may have made from soy powder or soy flour is, by comparison to the kind you are about to make, not quite fit to drink.

The benefits of making soy milk are numerous. It is fresh and sweet because you make it yourself. It is equivalent to dairy milk in almost every respect. Soy milk is excellent for people on special diets, or for people who cannot tolerate cow's milk. It is about 4 percent fat, compared to about 3.5 percent for dairy milk. Unlike dairy milk, however, soy milk has no cholesterol at all.

And to top it off, you can make up to 7 quarts of soy milk from a pound of beans. If the beans cost as much as $1 a pound, the milk would still cost less than 15 cents a quart.

Soy milk can be used instead of cow's milk in every recipe calling for milk: in cream sauces, soups, sauces, puddings and custards, beverages, and baking.

Its most serious fault is that it is low in calcium. If you use soy milk for all your milk needs, you must remember to use a calcium supplement. It can be added to the milk, but I suggest taking it separately, since calcium compounds will curdle soy milk.

ABOUT SOLIDIFIERS

The recipe for making tofu follows that for making soy milk. The same equipment is used for both. Tofu calls for one additional ingredient, a solidifier or curdling agent. The most easily obtained is ordinary Epsom salts. So little is used that one pound will probably last a year or more.

You may have noticed, if you are a label reader, that some store-bought tofu will say "Made with Natural Nigari," and others will merely list "Calcium Sulfate" as an ingredient. These are the most commonly used solidifiers for commercial tofu. You can use them, too, but they are harder to find. Some health food stores may have one or the other, but neither is necessary if you have Epsom salts.

When a dairy makes cheese from cow's milk it uses rennet to curdle the milk. Soy milk will not curdle with rennet; other substances must be used. Nigari is one, Epsom salts is another, Calcium sulfate is a third. Lemon juice and vinegar work, too, but make a sour tasting tofu.

Nigari is a by-product of the manufacture of sea salt. The English word for it is *bittern*; nigari is the Japanese name and until very recently all of it came from Japan— from the Sea of Japan. It is magnesium chloride. It is expensive.

Epsom salts is a common compound found in every drugstore and most supermarkets. It is used for bathing, soaking the feet, and as a laxative. It is magnesium sulfate. It is very cheap.

Both of these compounds make light, sweet tofu. Both have magnesium in common. Very little of either is used in making tofu, but some people are extremely sensitive to magnesium and are unable to tolerate even a tiny bit. Very little of the solidifier remains in the tofu, but that can be too much for some folks.

Calcium sulfate is another solidifier, the one I greatly prefer. It is also called gypsum, and it is a perfectly natural substance. The kind used by commercial tofu-makers is pharmaceutically pure. It has the distinct advantage of producing tofu that is rich in calcium. It makes the lightest, sweetest and most velvety tofu. While it is also very inexpensive, unfortunately, it is difficult to obtain.

Lemon juice and vinegar will also make tofu from soy milk. I find the taste of this tofu rather unpleasant and never use either. If used, you will, of course, taste them.

I make a big point of discussing the solidifiers when I teach tofu-making classes. There is so much folderol and mystique about anything labeled "natural" these days, that we are apt to think anything not so labeled is bad. It is just not true. I feel very strongly that people are still able to improve on nature. I think tofu is a distinct improvement over dry soybeans.

ABOUT EQUIPMENT . . .

You need *no* curious, exotic, or special equipment for making soy milk and tofu. The most ordinary American kitchen will have just about everything. You will need:

1. A very large pot, such as a stock pot or canning pot, about 12- to 16-quart capacity, preferably with a heavy bottom. If you have a thin metal pan, elevate it from the heat with a metal trivet or an asbestos pad.

2. A pressing cloth made of a 24-inch square of a fine mesh material, cotton or synthetic, but strong. The ordinary cheesecloth found in most stores will not do. It will not last and is not strong enough. Some curtain materials are excellent; gauzy materials are also very

good, the kind used in light, summer clothing. Unbleached muslin is not good, unless it is loosely woven. Gauze diapers are great.

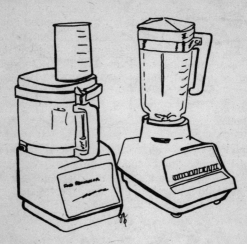

3. An electric blender for grinding the beans. A food processor will also work, or a juicing machine. Hand grinders also work; a good food mill can also be used.
4. A large colander (metal or plastic).

5. Measuring cups, measuring spoons, miscellaneous bowls, rubber spatulas, large spoons, etc.
6. A mold with a capacity of about 2 quarts. This is the most highly specialized piece of equipment, one you may not yet find in the stores. I use a nested colander/bowl set made of plastic and find it efficient and useful for other things besides tofu-making. You can improvise with anything from an ordinary colander to a plastic container. Two things are very important:

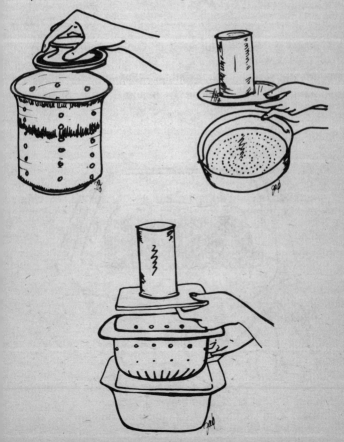

1. *The mold must have lots of holes on the bottom and up the sides*
2. *You must have a flat lid that fits INSIDE the mold with ¼-inch clearance all around. A plate will do for round molds. (I cut mine to fit out of masonite and wrapped it in foil.)*

SOY MILK

7 quarts

1 pound dry soybeans (or about 7½ cups soaked soybeans)
28 cups of water

Wash the beans and soak them overnight. Add water for soaking to 3 inches above the beans. They must soak for at least 10 hours.

In the morning, drain the beans and wash them again. (Marvel a bit at how large they have grown.)

Apply a no-stick spray to a large pot, one with a capacity of at least 12 quarts.

Set the pan over medium to high heat and put 2 cups of

water into the pot. *Start now to keep track of the amount of WATER and the number of cups of SOAKED BEANS.* This cannot be overemphasized. You have just used 2 cups of water. Write it down.

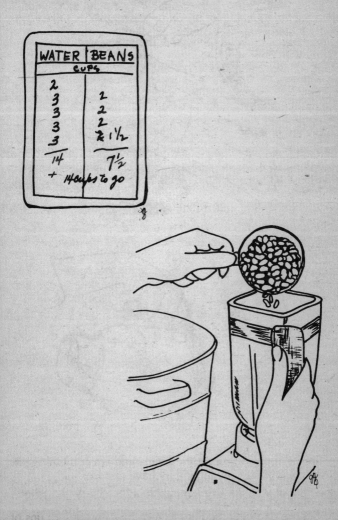

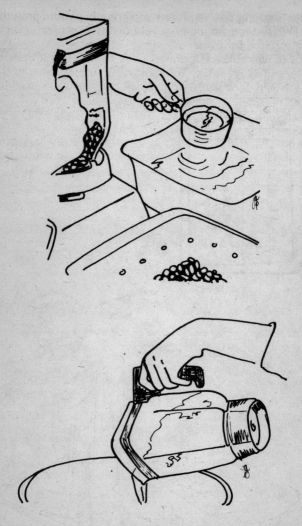

Combine 3 cups of water with 2 cups of soaked beans in a blender jar or in a food processor. (If you are using a grinder or a food mill or a juicer, use the instructions for your machine and add water accordingly.) Grind until the beans solids are about the size of coarse cornmeal. Add to the cooking pot.

Continue grinding, using 3 cups of water to 2 cups of beans, until the beans are all ground, adding them to the pot as you go. Keep a running total of the water used for grinding and the cups of soaked beans.

Bring the soybean-water mixture to a full boil, then reduce the heat and cook the mash at a simmer for 20 to 30 minutes. This long cooking time is necessary to destroy a substance in soybeans called the "trypsin inhibitor," which prevents the body from assimilating soy protein.

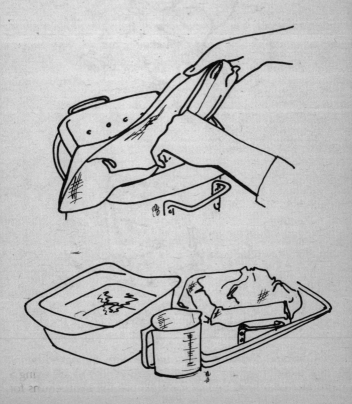

While the mash cooks, place a colander over a pot or large bowl in the sink. When working with hot liquids I think it is safest to work in the sink. Wet the pressing cloth and drape it evenly over the colander. Measure remainder of water to be used into a bowl and set it aside.

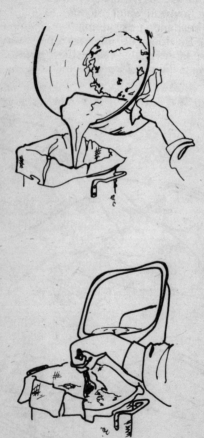

When the mash has cooked, pour it into the cloth-lined colander. Pour the remainder of the water (about 14 cups) through the mash, stirring to cool. Gather the corners of the cloth together and twist until all of the water is squeezed out of the mash. The solids left in the cloth are called "okara," and this has very special uses that will be discussed later.

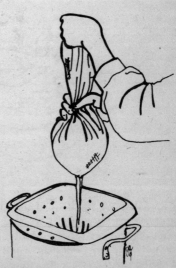

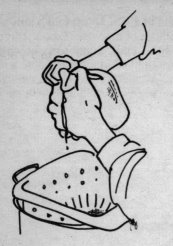

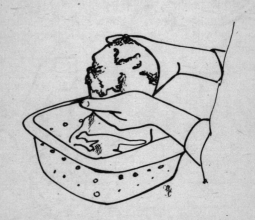

You will now have used about 28 cups of water; 14 during the grinding and cooking process and another 14 to cool the mash so that it can be handled to press out all the water. The soy milk is now finished and can be bottled and refrigerated. You can bottle a quart or two and use the rest for making tofu, if you wish.

MAKING TOFU WITH EPSOM SALTS OR NIGARI

2½ to 3½ pounds

Prepare the soy milk according to the instructions above. Place it over medium heat, elevated if necessary to prevent burning. Bring to a boil. While it is heating mix the solidifier.

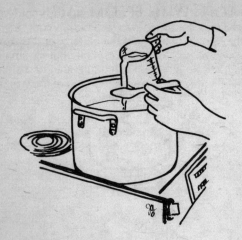

To 2 cups water add
2½ teaspoons Epsom salts OR
2½ teaspoons finely ground Nigari

Stir well and set aside until the soy milk boils. When the boiling point is reached, remove the pot from the heat. Add one-third of the solidifier to the pot and mix in very well. Stop the agitation by drawing a spoon very gently through the milk until the swirling stops. Then add another third, stirring very gently. Cover the pot and let it stand for 3 minutes. If the mixture has not curdled and separated into white clouds of curd and yellowish clear whey, add more solidifier, stirring gently until the separation is complete.

The amount of solidifier you will need depends very much on the kind of water in your area. Some water needs very little agent—others needs much more. It is not necessary to use all of the solidifier. When the curdling takes place, and the whey looks clear, or just very slightly milky, you have used enough. Throw the rest away. Let the tofu stand while you prepare the mold.

Rinse the pressing cloth well in cold water. Arrange it in the mold and set it in the sink, or, if you wish to save the whey, over a pot. Ladle the curds into the mold very gently. Agitation causes the tofu to lose bulk. Work slowly, letting the whey drain away. Fold the cloth over the curds. Cover with the flat lid, or with a plate that is smaller than the mold, and weight with a 1-pound can or a stone. Allow it to stand for about 10 minutes. Remove the weight.

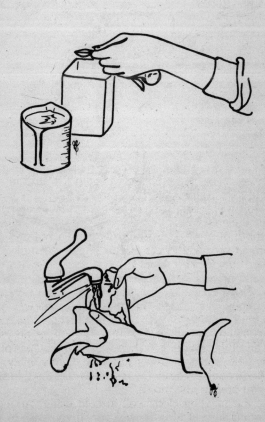

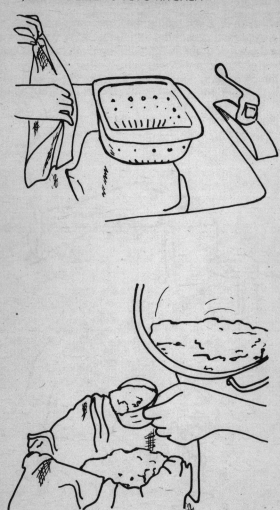

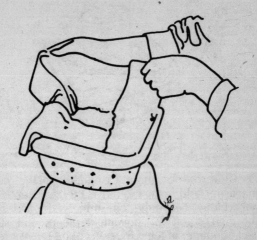

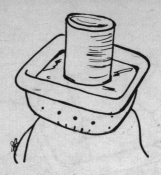

Cool the tofu for about 15 minutes in the mold, then immerse in cold water. Remove the mold and the cloth very carefully. Leave the tofu in the water as long as you wish, then cut it in convenient pieces and store in a closed container in the refrigerator. You may store it under water if you wish, or you may store it without water. It will keep for 1½ to 2 weeks (see page 6 for information about storage).

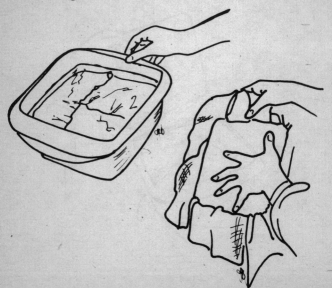

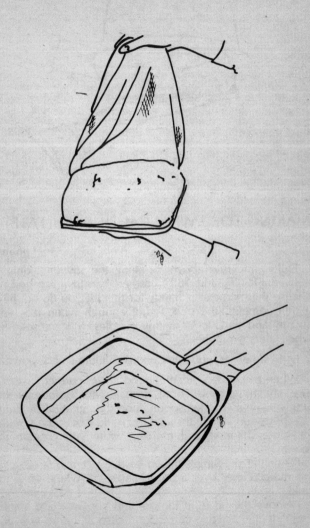

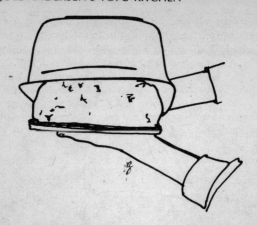

MAKING TOFU WITH CALCIUM SULFATE

3 to 4 pounds

Follow the rule above, bringing the soy milk only to between 170°F. and 180°F. rather than to a full boil. (A cheese thermometer is handy for this.) If you do not have a thermometer, the milk is hot enough when it is very steamy and starts to show tiny bubbles. Mix the solidifier while the soymilk heats:

To 1 cup water, add 2 teaspoons calcium sulfate powder

When the milk is steaming and at the correct temperature, stir in the solidifier all at once. Mix thoroughly, but gently, with a wooden spoon. Stop the agitation by drawing the spoon slowly through the milk. Cover the pot and let it stand for several minutes while you prepare the mold.

Rinse the pressing cloth in cold water and arrange in the mold, either over a pot to catch the whey, or in the sink.

Remove the lid from the pot and you will find a solid mass. If you have ever made cheese at home you will recognize this curd. You must release the whey from the curd; this is done by making cuts in the mass with a long, stainless-steel knife. Cut through making a 1-inch grid. Then slant the knife and cut both the length and width at a diagonal. You will see the whey begin to separate from the curds. Set the pot by the sink and let it stand for 5 minutes, then gently ladle the curds and whey into the mold. Do this slowly, allowing the whey to run off. Fold the cloth over the curds, weight with a cover or plate and a 1-pound weight for 10 to 20 minutes. Place the whole mold in cold water for about 10 minutes and then carefully remove the mold and the cloth. Cut into convenient pieces and store in a closed container. Refrigerate (see storage instructions on page 6).

RICH SOY MILK

You can make a thicker, richer soy milk by using less water. If you would like to make 2 quarts of rich milk use:

1 cup dry soybeans (3 cups soaked)
8 cups water
Follow the rule for making soy milk above.

MILDER TASTING SOY MILK

An alternative method for making soy milk involves grinding the beans in boiling water. This will hasten the cooking process because the mash will be boiling by the time you finish grinding the beans. This can be slow death to plastic blender jars, which develop tiny crack marks from the heat. There is no advantage other than making a soy milk that some say tastes better.

ALL ABOUT OKARA

When you make tofu or soy milk you will also make okara; it can't be helped. Okara is the Japanese word used to describe the high fiber, solid part of the soybean that is left after you press the soy milk. Remove it from the pressing cloth, store it in a plastic container in the refrigerator. It will keep as long as the soy milk or tofu you have made at the same time.

Okara has many uses, but is most useful in baked goods. It adds fiber, texture, and protein without altering the flavor or color of the food. It serves a similar use as bran, but bran colors and flavors and has little protein.

Use okara in breads, cakes, pie crusts and pastries, waffles and pancakes, and muffins.

Add it to tofuburger, too. Use as an extender with meat, fish, or poultry. If you make your own pet foods it will supply fiber and protein. If you run out of food uses, dig it into your garden.

A LITTLE ABOUT WHEY

If you have made tofu and have caught the whey in a pot, you probably expect to use it for something. It has some definite uses, but there are some things you ought to know.

Whey contains most of the solidifier used in making the tofu. It also contains much of the carbohydrate from the soybean and a lot of what it is about beans (in general) that causes gas. With this in mind, you can use the whey in a few ways.

Whey is just great in making yeast breads. It makes the yeast just dance. It adds some protein and acts as a dough conditioner. It can be used as a soup base or a water for cooking vegetables. Pets seem to like to drink it; it gives them gas, too.

It has non-food uses too. You can wash up your tofu equipment with it. I have been told that it lends a beautiful sheen to wooden floors. It is good for the garden, but don't use it on house plants. (It will mold and kill the roots in confined pots.)

3
SALAD DRESSINGS, DIPS, APPETIZERS, AND SAUCES

Making creamy salad dressings is so easy with tofu. Most of the dressings can be used as dips, or spreads for sandwiches, or for appetizers. It is all a matter of how thick or how thin you make the mixture and in what part of the meal you choose to serve it.

Firm tofu can be used as a refreshing and delightful appetizer. Just cut it in cubes and serve it as is. A pile of fresh, white tofu cubes, a dipping sauce or two, and a package of toothpicks to use as spears will contribute to conversation and to the well-being of your guests.

LEMON SPICE DRESSING

1½ cups

½ cup soft stofu
½ lemon, unpeeled and
  cut in pieces
1 teaspoon curry powder
1 teaspoon paprika
2 cloves garlic, or 1
  teaspoon garlic
  powder

¼ teaspoon sugar
½ teaspoon salt
¼ cup salad oil
¼ to ½ cup white wine or
  water to thin

Combine all the ingredients except the wine or water in a blender jar or food processor bowl and puree until very smooth. Add wine to thin to desired consistency. Allow to stand for several hours to meld flavors before using.

GREEN GODDESS DRESSING

About 2 cups

½ cup parsley sprigs
2 whole green onions
1 cup soft tofu
¼ cup yogurt
1½ tablespoons vinegar
1 teaspoon Worcestershire
   sauce

½ (2-ounce) can anchovy
   fillets
¼ teaspoon pepper
Salt to taste
Soy milk, dairy milk, or
   water to thin

Chop the parsley and green onion in a blender or food processor. Add the tofu, yogurt, vinegar, Worcestershire sauce, anchovies, and pepper and blend until very smooth. Taste and add salt, if needed. Thin to desired consistency.

CREAMY GARLIC DRESSING

1 cup

2 cloves garlic
1 tablespoon lemon juice
   or vinegar
1 teaspoon Worcestershire
   sauce

¼ teaspoon salt
1 cup soft tofu
2 tablespoons grated strong
   cheese
¼ cup salad oil

Combine the garlic, lemon juice, Worcestershire sauce, and salt in a blender jar and blend until garlic is liquefied. Add the tofu and cheese and continue blending until the dressing is very smooth. Thin with water, if necessary.

Add the oil in a thin stream. This will thicken the dressing considerably. Use for green salads or, if thick, as a dip or spread.

SHRIMP APPETIZER OR DRESSING

2 cups

1 cup soft tofu, mashed
¼ cup yogurt
1 tablespoon lemon juice or vinegar
½ teaspoon salt
1 cup cooked shrimp, or 1 7-ounce can of shrimp, cut in small pieces

½ teaspoon paprika
2 tablespoons chopped green onion, or 1 tablespoon dried onion flakes
2 tablespoons chopped celery
1 teaspoon celery seeds

Combine the tofu, yogurt, lemon juice, and salt in a bowl and mix well. Add the remaining ingredients. Thin with water if necessary.

Chill for several hours or overnight before serving. Serve with crisp vegetables or chips.

Note: Add additional water to make an excellent salad dressing.

CRAB APPETIZER

2½ cups

1 cup soft tofu, mashed
¼ cup sour cream or yogurt
1 tablespoon lemon juice
½ teaspoon salt, or to taste
½ teaspoon pepper

½ teaspoon garlic powder
1 cup flaked crabmeat, or 1 7-ounce can crabmeat, flaked

Combine tofu, sour cream, lemon juice, salt, pepper, and garlic powder in a blender or food processor bowl and process. Transfer to another bowl and stir in the crabmeat. Refrigerate for several hours before serving.

BAGNA CAUDA
(Anchovy Dip)

1½ cups

6 tablespoons butter or margarine

2 cloves garlic, finely mashed

1 2-ounce can anchovy fillets

1 tablespoon cold water (approximately)

1 teaspoon cornstarch

½ cup soft tofu

1 tablespoon lemon juice

Melt 2 tablespoons of the butter in a skillet and add the garlic. Sauté for three minutes and then add the anchovies. Mash the anchovies and garlic together and remove from heat.

Combine the water, cornstarch, tofu, and lemon juice in the food processor bowl and puree until very smooth. If it is too thick, add more water. Melt the remaining 4 tablespoons butter and add to the tofu mixture in a thin stream.

Transfer the mixture to a bowl and stir in the anchovy mixture. Serve warm in a fondue pot over heat, or serve warm just after mixing. This is delicious with chunks of fresh vegetables such as mushrooms, zucchini, cauliflower, broccoli, tomato, or avocado. It can also be served with bread chunks or chips.

Note: This dip does not improve with age.

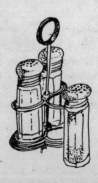

SPINACH DIP

3 cups

- 1 small bunch fresh, raw spinach, washed well and chopped
- ½ cup chopped green onion
- ½ cup chopped fresh parsley
- 1 cup soft tofu
- ½ cup yogurt
- 2 tablespoons lemon juice
- 1 teaspoon dry mustard
- 1 teaspoon salt
- ½ teaspoon sugar
- ¼ teaspoon pepper
- ½ cup oil

Combine the spinach, onion, and parsley and chop very fine in a bowl or a food processor. Transfer to another bowl.

Combine the remaining ingredients in a blender jar or food processor and blend until very smooth. Stir into the spinach. Taste and correct the seasoning. Serve with fresh vegetable chunks.

GUACAMOLE

2 cups

- 1 soft avocado (a medium one gives about 1 cup of pulp)
- ½ cup soft tofu
- ¼ cup tofu mayonnaise (see page 47) or other mayonnaise
- 2 to 3 tablespoons lemon juice or vinegar, or to taste
- 2 teaspoons chili powder
- ½ teaspoon salt
  Hot pepper sauce or cayenne to taste
- 1 medium-sized tomato, chopped
- ¼ cup chopped green onion, or 2 tablespoons chopped onion
- 2 tablespoons chopped parsley

Peel the avocado and remove the pit. Combine in a bowl with the tofu and mash together. The mixture will be a bit lumpy. (If you like a smooth guacomole, process in a blender or food processor until very smooth.)

Add the mayonnaise, lemon juice, chili powder, salt,

and pepper sauce. Mix well and taste to correct seasoning.

Stir in the tomato, onion, and parsley. Refrigerate for an hour or so before serving with corn chips or unflavored tortilla chips.

CHILLED TOFU CUBES

1 12-ounce package firm tofu	Ice cubes Toothpicks

Cut the tofu into bite-sized cubes. Pile them in a decorative glass bowl. Place the bowl in a larger bowl filled with ice. Put the toothpicks in a small glass. Serve with any one of the dips that are in this section or with plain soy sauce or teriyaki sauce.

MARINATED TOFU CUBES

Serves 4

12 ounces (4 slices) firm tofu	½ teaspoon dried tarragon
⅓ cup wine or cider vinegar	1 teaspoon dried mint
	1 teaspoon salt
¼ cup olive or other oil	¼ teaspoon sugar
1 large clove garlic, pressed or mashed	1 medium onion, thinly sliced

Cut the tofu into ½- to ¾-inch cubes.

Combine the vinegar, oil, garlic, tarragon, mint, salt and sugar in a saucepan and bring to a boil. Reduce heat and simmer for 5 minutes. Strain and discard flavorings. Return to the heat and add the onion. Cover and simmer for 5 minutes.

Add the tofu cubes to the marinade and stir gently but thoroughly. Cover the pan and simmer for 5 minutes longer. Allow to cool, covered. Stir again before refrigerating in a glass or plastic container. Chill at least 2 days before serving.

Turn cubes into a bowl with the marinade. Use toothpicks as spears.

LEMON-GARLIC TOFU CUBES

Serves 4

12 ounces (4 slices) firm tofu
2 to 3 cloves garlic, mashed
¼ cup oil

¼ cup lemon juice
2 teaspoons dried mint leaves
½ to 1 teaspoon salt
Pepper to taste

Cut the tofu into ½- to ¾-inch cubes.

Over medium heat, sauté the garlic in the oil for three minutes, stirring and pressing the garlic with a fork. Remove the garlic and discard. Add the tofu cubes and cook, stirring, over low heat for 2 minutes. Remove from the heat and add the remaining ingredients.

Allow to cool at room temperature and then refrigerate for a day or so. The cubes are best when served at room temperature, but they need some time to mellow.

CREAMY TOFU
A mix for dips and salad dressings

About 1½ cups

1 cup soft tofu
¼ to ½ cup buttermilk, yogurt, soy milk, or dairy milk

1 to 3 tablespoons lemon juice or vinegar
½ to 1 teaspoon salt, or to taste

Combine the tofu, ¼ cup of the liquid, 1 tablespoon of lemon juice and ½ teaspoon salt in a blender jar and puree until very smooth. Add more liquid as needed, perhaps a mixture of milk and yogurt, to achieve the consistency of sour cream or thick yogurt. Add more lemon juice or vinegar, and salt to taste.

A little experience with this mix will be most rewarding, as you will learn for yourself just which flavor pleases you most.

Stored in the refrigerator, the mix will keep for about 2 weeks and taste better every day.

Using the Creamy Tofu above, you can make a great

number of dips. Most of these can also serve as delicious salad dressings. Add milk or water to the recipe and the dip becomes a salad dressing. The difference, then, between a dip and a dressing is in consistency.

Note: For a variety of flavors try these recipes

1. Blue Cheese   2 cups

1½ cups Creamy Tofu mix (see page 41)

1 small clove garlic, or ½ teaspoon garlic powder

2 to 3 ounces blue cheese, or to taste

Combine the ingredients in a blender or food processor bowl and blend until very smooth. Taste and correct the seasoning. If you like lumps of cheese, reserve part of the cheese to crumble and stir into the dressing after removing from the blender.

2. Garlic   1½ cups

2 to 4 cloves very fresh garlic

1½ cups Creamy Tofu mix (see page 41)

Using a sharp knife, chop the garlic very fine. Don't crush the garlic, as this releases more oils and makes a strong flavored dip without the crunch and the bite. Stir the garlic into the tofu mix and serve at once.

3. Onion or Scallion   About 2 cups

⅓ cup chopped fresh onion, scallions or chives

1½ cups Creamy Tofu mix (see page 41)

½ teaspoon Worcestershire sauce
Pepper to taste

Combine the ingredients and refrigerate for about 1 hour before serving.

4. Thousand Island   2 cups

1½ cups Creamy Tofu mix
(see page 41)
¼ cup catsup or chili sauce
½ teaspoon Worcestershire
sauce
½ teaspoon dry mustard
2 tablespoons sweet pickle
relish

2 tablespoons chopped dill
pickle
2 teaspoons dried chopped
onion
Salt and pepper

Combine tofu mix, catsup, Worcestershire sauce, and mustard and blend smooth. Stir in the relish, pickle and onion. Add salt and pepper to taste. Refrigerate for about 1 hour before serving.

5. Sour Pickle   About 2 cups

1½ cups Creamy Tofu mix
(see page 41)
¼ to ⅓ cup chopped dill
pickle

1 teaspoon white
horseradish
½ teaspoon celery seeds

Combine ingredients, blending thoroughly. Chill before serving.

6. Onion Soup Mix   2¼ cups

1½ cups Creamy Tofu mix
(see page 41)

1 package French onion
soup mix, or to taste

Stir the tofu and soup mixes together. Refrigerate for at least an hour before serving. (These soup mixes get very strong as they stand, so be careful how much you use.)

7. Horseradish   1 cup

1 cup Creamy Tofu mix
(see page 41)

1 teaspoon to 1 tablespoon
white horseradish

Stir tofu mix and horseradish together. How much horseradish you add is a matter of taste. Some like it hot! This is excellent served with roast meats.

8. Creamy French   1 cup

½ cup Creamy Tofu mix   2 teaspoons paprika
   (see page 41)   1 clove garlic
2 tablespoons wine vinegar   ½ teaspoon salt
¼ cup salad oil   ¼ teaspoon pepper

Combine all the ingredients in a blender jar. Blend smooth.
Add water to thin, if necessary.

9. Dill   1½ cups

1½ cups Creamy Tofu mix   1 tablespoon dill weed
   (see page 41)   ¼ teaspoon pepper

Blend the ingredients. Refrigerate for several hours before
serving to develop the dill flavor.

10. Clam   2½ cups

2 cups Creamy Tofu mix   1 teaspoon Worcestershire
   (see page 41)   sauce
1 can minced clams,   ¼ teaspoon salt (if needed)
   drained (save liquid for   Pepper to taste
   another use)
2 tablespoons chopped
   scallions or chives

Combine the tofu mix, clams, scallions, and Worcestershire sauce. Taste and add salt and pepper as needed.
Chill before serving.

11. Curry-Olive   1½ cups

1½ cups Creamy Tofu mix   1 to 3 teaspoons curry
   (see page 41)   powder, to taste
1 2-ounce to 4-ounce small   1 teaspoon dried chopped
   can black chopped olives   onion

Combine the ingredients. Chill before serving.

12. Tarragon and Mustard   1½-plus cups

1½ cups Creamy Tofu mix   ½ to 1 teaspoon dried
   (see page 41)   tarragon leaves
2 to 4 tablespoons Dijon   2 teaspoons lemon juice
   mustard   Salt and pepper to taste

Mix the creamy tofu, mustard, tarragon, and lemon juice together and refrigerate for an hour or so. Add salt and pepper to taste.

13. Lemon-Garlic   1½ cups

½ whole lemon, unpeeled
1 clove garlic
1 to 2 teaspoons curry powder
½ teaspoon paprika

1 teaspoon mustard
1 cup Creamy Tofu Mix (see page 41)
Hot pepper sauce (optional)

Cut the lemon in small pieces. Combine the lemon, garlic, curry powder, paprika, mustard, and tofu mix in a blender jar and blend until very smooth. Add pepper sauce to taste. Refrigerate to allow flavors to meld.

14. Sesame-Garlic   1½ cups

1 cup Creamy Tofu mix (see page 41)
¼ cup tahini (ground sesame seeds)
1 tablespoon lemon juice

1 large clove garlic
¼ cup yogurt
¼ teaspoon salt
Hot pepper sauce to taste

Combine the tofu mix, tahini, lemon juice, garlic, and yogurt in a blender and blend until smooth. Add salt and hot pepper sauce as desired. Refrigerate for an hour or so before serving.

TOFU SAUCES

Tofu is unparalleled for making sauces of all kinds. As an ingredient, it can replace eggs, cream, and milk. Tofu is especially valuable when used to make such sauces as mayonnaise, hollandaise, and béarnaise. It is a natural emulsifier as it can take up and hold droplets of fat in suspension, which is the secret of these sauces.

Nutritionally, mayonnaise, hollandaise, and béarnaise have a bad reputation—too much cholesterol, too many calories. Making these sauces with tofu instead of eggs reduces the cholesterol greatly. Then, if you use margarine or oil instead of butter, the cholesterol is further reduced.

Calories can be reduced by using more tofu and less oil, with results that are nearly as good. A rule for this is: For each 1 tablespoon reduction of oil in any recipe, add 1 tablespoon of tofu.

Making these sauces with tofu virtually eliminates the problem of the curdling that can happen when eggs are used. If some separation does occur, just a little more blending will correct it.

HOLLANDAISE SAUCE

1½ cups

½ cup soft tofu
2 tablespoons lemon juice
¼ teaspoon salt

Pinch of cayenne
½ to ⅔ cup melted, hot butter

Combine the tofu, lemon juice, salt, and cayenne in a blender jar. Have the butter ready. Start the tofu mixture at low speed and increase to the highest speed. Add the butter by droplets at first, and then increase to a steady stream.

The sauce should be served immediately, without reheating. There is seldom a failure when using tofu instead of eggs. If there should be some separation of fat, reblend but do not heat.

BÉARNAISE SAUCE

1½ cups

¼ cup dry white wine
1 tablespoon minced onion
½ teaspoon dried tarragon
¼ cup wine vinegar
¼ teaspoon salt

¼ teaspoon pepper
1 teaspoon chopped parsley
½ cup soft tofu
¾ cup melted butter

Combine the wine, onion, tarragon, vinegar, salt, pepper, and parsley in a small saucepan and cook over high heat until reduced by half. Strain this mixture into a blender jar and add the tofu. Blend until very smooth.

While blending at medium speed, add about half the butter by droplets. Increase the speed and add the butter in a slow, steady stream. Serve at once.

CHORON SAUCE

This is especially good with baked tofu slices.　　2 cups

¼ cup white wine
¼ cup wine vinegar
1 tablespoon minced onion
½ teaspoon dried tarragon
½ teaspoon salt
¼ teaspoon pepper
1 teaspoon chopped parsley

½ cup soft tofu
3 tablespoons tomato sauce or puree
¾ cup melted hot butter or margarine

Combine the wine, vinegar, onion, tarragon, salt, pepper, and parsley in a saucepan and boil until it is reduced by half. Strain this mixture into a blender jar. Add the tofu and the tomato sauce and blend until smooth.

Add the hot butter by droplets while blending at high speed. As it becomes thicker, continue in a stream. It will be thick and creamy. Serve at once.

TOFU MAYONNAISE

2 cups

½ cup soft tofu
1 teaspoon mustard (dry or prepared)
1 teaspoon salt
3 tablespoons mild vinegar or lemon juice

¼ teaspoon white pepper
1 teaspoon sugar
1 cup oil

Combine the tofu, mustard, salt, 1 tablespoon of the vinegar, pepper, sugar and ¼ cup of the oil in a blender and puree until very smooth. Then, while blending at high speed, add ¼ cup of oil in droplets. Add the remaining 2 tablespoons of vinegar, slowly. Then add the last ½ cup of oil in a fine stream.

If the mixture is very thick and refuses to blend more, omit the last ½ cup of oil and use the mayonnaise as is. It will not make a bit of difference and you will have saved lots of calories.

Sauces based on mayonnaise can be made with tofu mayonnaise; try some of the following.

MAYONNAISE SAUCES

1. Seafood Sauce   1 cup

1 cup tofu mayonnaise (see page 47)
3 tablespoons catsup
2 teaspoons lemon juice
1 teaspoon horseradish
¼ cup pickle relish or chopped dill pickle
½ teaspoon salt
Pepper to taste

Combine all the ingredients. Taste and correct seasoning. Serve with shrimp, crabmeat, lobster, or other cold seafoods.

2. Curry Sauce   1 cup

1 cup tofu mayonnaise (see page 47)
2 teaspoons curry powder
1 teaspoon vinegar
½ teaspoon onion powder
¼ teaspoon salt
¼ teaspoon pepper
Cayenne or Tabasco (optional)

Combine all the ingredients, mixing well. Serve with fish cakes or vegetables—hot or cold.

3. Mustard Sauce   1 cup

1 cup tofu mayonnaise (see page 47)
2 teaspoons mustard
½ teaspoon dried tarragon
1 tablespoon chopped parsley
¼ teaspoon salt
Pepper to taste

Combine all the ingredients. Serve with vegetables and meat and fish dishes.

4. Caper Sauce   1 cup

½ cup tofu mayonnaise
(see page 47)
½ cup yogurt
1 teaspoon lemon juice
½ teaspoons salt

¼ teaspoon pepper
1 tablespoon chopped
chives or green onion
1 tablespoon parsley
2 tablespoons capers

Combine the mayonnaise, yogurt, lemon juice, salt, and pepper in a blender jar and blend until smooth. Mix in the chives, parsley, and capers. Chill for several hours before serving with fish or seafood.

LEARNING TREE MAYONNAISE

½ cup oil
1 small clove garlic
⅛ to ¼ cup onion
2 tablespoons lemon juice
2 teaspoons cider vinegar

1 teaspoon salt
¼ to ½ tablespoon
Dijon-type mustard
2 cups soft tofu

Combine the oil, garlic, onion, lemon juice, vinegar, salt, and mustard in a blender jar or food processor bowl and blend until the onion and garlic are liquefied. Add the tofu and whip until very smooth.

Note: You may like to vary the amount of onion and other flavorings in this recipe. It should not have a pronounced onion flavor—but the onion gives the mayonnaise character.

Larry Needleman of The Learning Tree Company in California has perfected this recipe.

LEMON SAUCE

2 cups

¼ lemon, unpeeled
¼ cup salad oil
1 cup soft tofu
½ cup yogurt

1 teaspoon horseradish
1 teaspoon Dijon mustard
½ teaspoon salt

Cut the lemon in pieces and put in a blender jar with the oil. Blend until the lemon is chopped in tiny pieces. Add the remaining ingredients and blend until very smooth. Chill and serve as a dip or as a dressing for artichokes.

HORSERADISH SAUCE FOR FISH

1 cup

½ cup soft tofu
¼ cup yogurt
1 teaspoon vinegar
1 tablespoon white
horseradish

¼ to ⅓ cup reduced fish
stock or clam juice
Salt to taste

Combine the tofu, yogurt, vinegar, and horseradish in a blender jar and blend until smooth. Add the fish stock or clam juice to thin to desired consistency. Taste and add salt as needed. Serve with fish or fish-flavored tofuburgers (see pages 68, 73–75).

This very simple sauce is the basis for a thousand culinary delights. It is embarrassingly bland, but will take to flavors like a fish to water.

WHITE SAUCE

1 cup

¼ cup soft tofu
¾ cup cold water
1 teaspoon cornstarch
1 teaspoon salad oil

¼ teaspoon salt, or to taste
Pepper to taste
½ teaspoon lemon juice

Combine the tofu, water, cornstarch, oil, salt, and pepper, in a blender jar and blend until very smooth. Pour into a heavy-bottom saucepan and cook over medium heat, stirring constantly. When it has thickened, add the lemon juice and stir well.

Flavor the basic White Sauce with these variations:

1. Cheese Sauce

½ cup grated cheese (Cheddar, Swiss, or your choice)	1 cup White Sauce (see page 50) Hot water or milk to thin as needed
½ teaspoon Worcestershire sauce ·	

Add the cheese and Worcestershire sauce to the white sauce and stir until the cheese melts. If the sauce is too thick, thin to taste with hot water or milk.

2. Brown Onion Sauce

1 tablespoon oil	¼ teaspoon salt
1 large onion, chopped fairly fine	1 cup White Sauce (see page 50)

Heat the oil in a heavy-bottom skillet. Add the onion and the salt and fry until the onion is very brown, almost to the point of burning. Mix in the white sauce and serve piping hot with your choice of tofuburger (pages 65 to 75).

3. Horseradish Sauce

1 to 2 teaspoons white horseradish	1 teaspoon lemon juice
1 cup White Sauce (see page 50)	

Combine the ingredients, blending thoroughly. Serve hot with meats or baked tofu slices.

4. Curry Sauce

- 1 tablespoon dried chopped onion
- 2 teaspoons lemon juice
- 1 teaspoon to 1 tablespoon curry powder, or to taste
- 1 cup White Sauce (see page 50)

Combine all the ingredients. Taste and correct seasoning. Serve hot with tofu slices or with tofuburgers.

4. Mustard Sauce

- 1 cup White Sauce (see page 50)
- 1 teaspoon or more of prepared mustard
- ½ teaspoon celery seeds
- ½ teaspoon lemon juice

Combine all the ingredients. Serve with tofu slices or over hard-cooked eggs.

CREAMY WHITE SAUCE FOR FISH

1 cup

- ¼ cup soft tofu
- ¾ cup fish stock or clam juice
- 1 teaspoon cornstarch
- 1 teaspoon oil
- ½ teaspoon salt
- ¼ teaspoon pepper
- ¼ teaspoon horseradish or lemon juice

Combine all the ingredients in a blender jar and blend until very smooth. Transfer to a saucepan and cook, stirring constantly, until it thickens. Serve over fish fillets.

4

SALADS AND SANDWICHES

There are few better ways to use tofu than in salads and sandwiches. The recipes in this section are mostly for cold preparations to be eaten with lunch, as lunch, or for hot weather suppers.

I find the idea of the tofu being both in the salads or sandwich fixings and on them to be intriguing. There are few foods that have such versatility.

GREEN GODDESS MOLD

Serves 8

1 envelope (1 tablespoon) unflavored gelatin
1 cup boiling water
½ cup fresh parsley sprigs
2 or 3 whole green onions
1 tablespoon lemon juice
½ teaspoon salt
1 clove garlic (optional)
¼ teaspoon pepper
2 teaspoons prepared mustard
½ (2-ounce) can anchovy fillets
1 cup soft tofu
Drops of hot pepper sauce (optional)
1 ripe avocado, peeled and cut in pieces

Oil a 4-cup mold. Dissolve the gelatin completely in the boiling water. In a food processor or blender, combine the parsley, onion, lemon juice, salt, garlic, pepper, mustard, and anchovies. Add some of gelatin mixture to make the chopping easier. Chop very fine.

Add the tofu, pepper sauce, and the remaining water-gelatin mixture. Blend until very smooth. Taste and correct the seasoning.

You can add the avocado to the mixture and blend until

smooth, or fold in the avocado chunks. Either way is good.

Pour the mixture into the prepared mold. Refrigerate for several hours or overnight. Serve as a molded salad or a spread for bread or crackers.

CREAMY SEAFOOD MOLD

Serves 8

1 8-ounce bottle of clam juice
1 envelope (1 tablespoon) unflavored gelatin
2 tablespoons lemon juice
2 teaspoons prepared mustard
1 teaspoon prepared horseradish
¼ cup tomato catsup or tomato sauce
1 cup soft tofu
Salt and pepper
1 cup flaked fish, shrimp pieces, or any seafood
¼ cup thinly sliced celery
¼ cup thinly sliced green onion
¼ cup chopped green pepper

Oil a 4-cup mold. Heat the clam juice to a near boil and add the gelatin, stirring until gelatin is dissolved. Combine the lemon juice, mustard, horseradish, catsup, and tofu in a blender jar or food processor. Add as much of the gelatin mixture as needed to blend very smooth. Then add the remaining gelatin-clam juice and blend until well mixed. Add salt and pepper to taste.

Pour into a bowl and stir in the fish, celery, onion, and green pepper. Transfer to the prepared mold and refrigerate for several hours or overnight. Serve as the main course of a cold summer meal, garnished with salad vegetables and accompanied by other salads, a chilled white wine, and fresh French bread.

MOLDED VEGETABLE SALAD

Serves 6 to 8

1½ cups consommé,
  bouillon, or other clear
  soup
1 envelope (1 tablespoon)
  unflavored gelatin
2 tablespoons lemon juice
  or vinegar
1 teaspoon Dijon mustard
1 teaspoon dried tarragon

1 2-ounce to 4-ounce can
  chopped black olives,
  drained
1½ cups diced cooked or
  raw vegetables or a
  combination
¼ cup diced pickle, sweet
  or sour
1 cup of ½-inch cubes soft
  or firm tofu

Heat 1 cup of the soup to boiling. Add the gelatin and stir until the gelatin dissolves. Add the lemon juice, mustard, tarragon, and the remaining ½ cup of soup. Stir until the mustard is well dispersed (you may have to use the blender for this). Chill until the mixture is partly set, about 1 hour. Oil a 5-inch × 9-inch bread pan.

Fold in the olives, vegetables, pickles, and tofu cubes. If you are using soft tofu, stir very carefully in order not to crush them. Turn into the prepared pan and refrigerate for several hours or overnight.

Serve as a salad with a garnish of tomato slices or as the main course of a luncheon.

DUTCH POTATO SALAD

5 cups

2 pounds medium-sized
  potatoes (6 to 8)
⅔ cup chopped onion
1½ teaspoons salt
2 tablespoons chopped
  fresh parsley
½ teaspoon celery seeds

3 to 4 slices of bacon
⅓ cup vinegar
  Bacon drippings
1 tablespoon sugar
3 tablespoons water
¼ cup soft tofu
½ teaspoon pepper

Cook the potatoes in boiling, salted water until tender. Cool slightly, peel, and slice or dice.

While potatoes are cooking, combine the onion with 1 teaspoon of the salt and set aside for at least 10 minutes (the salt draws out the harsh flavors). Wash the onions thoroughly before combining with the potatoes, parsley, and celery seeds.

Dice the bacon and fry until very crisp. Drain and reserve the fat. Combine the vinegar, bacon fat, ½ teaspoon salt, sugar, water, tofu, and pepper in the blender and blend smooth to make a dressing.

Pour this dressing over the potatoes. Add the bacon and mix lightly. Serve warm.

TUNA AND CHEESE SANDWICH

6 sandwiches

1	6½-ounce can tuna		Salt and pepper to taste
1	tablespoon dried chopped onion	3	English muffins, halved and toasted
1	tablespoon lemon juice	6	slices Cheddar or American cheese
¼	cup chopped celery		
½	cup tofu mayonnaise (see page 47)	6	tomato slices

Drain and flake the tuna. Combine with the onion, lemon juice, celery, and tofu mayonnaise, mixing well. Taste and add salt and pepper, if needed.

Pile on the muffin halves and top with a slice of cheese. Heat under the broiler just long enough to melt the cheese, but not long enough to heat the tuna salad. Serve with a tomato slice.

SAVORY TOFU SANDWICH SPREAD

Serves 4 to 6

1 12-ounce package firm
   tofu
1 teaspoon onion powder
½ teaspoon garlic powder
1 to 1½ teaspoons beau
   monde or Greek
   seasoning
1 teaspoon paprika

2 teaspoons lemon juice
2 tablespoons poppy seeds
½ to 1 teaspoon salt, or to
   taste
½ teaspoon pepper
   (optional)
2 to 4 tablespoons yogurt
   or buttermilk to thin

Mash the tofu with a fork or potato masher. Add the onion and garlic powders, seasoning, paprika, lemon juice, and poppy seeds. Mix well and then taste before adding salt and pepper. Thin to a desired texture with yogurt or buttermilk. Refrigerate for several hours or overnight before using.

Serve on whole-grain bread with a leaf of lettuce. Simple and delicious!

TOFU SPREAD
A spread for sandwiches that has the texture of cream cheese.

1½ cups

8 ounces (about 1 cup)
   firm tofu
3 tablespoons yogurt or
   mayonnaise
1 tablespoon lemon juice

½ teaspoon mustard
½ teaspoon salt
Pepper to taste
1 tablespoon salad oil
   (optional)

Mash the tofu with a potato masher or a fork and add yogurt, lemon juice, mustard, salt, pepper, and oil. Add water in small amounts to achieve the desired consistency. Taste and correct seasoning.

Try these variations:

1. Tuna Curry or Catsup Spread   3 cups

- 1 6½-ounce can tuna fish
- 1 recipe tofu spread (see page 57)
- 1 teaspoon lemon juice
- ½ cup chopped celery
- 2 tablespoons chopped onion, or 1 tablespoon dry onion

- 1 to 2 teaspoons curry powder or 2 tablespoons tomato catsup
- Salt to taste

Drain the tuna and flake with a fork. Add to tofu spread with the lemon juice, celery, onion, and either the curry powder or catsup. Mix well and then taste. Add salt, if needed. Serve with lettuce on a toasted bun.

2. Fresh Zucchini Spread   1½ cups

- ½ cup chopped zucchini
- 2 tablespoons sunflower seeds or chopped nuts
- 1 small clove garlic, chopped very fine

- ½ teaspoon horseradish
- 1 cup tofu spread (see page 57)
- Salt and pepper to taste

Combine zucchini, seeds, garlic, horseradish and tofu spread, blending well. Add salt and pepper to taste. This is delicious as either a spread for bread or rolls, or as a salad.

3. Crunchy Tofu Spread   3½ cups

- 1 recipe tofu spread (see page 57)
- 1½ cups chopped vegetables (cucumber, mushrooms, bean sprouts, scallions, pea pods, carrots, peas, cauliflower, green beans, beets, or any combination of fresh or cooked vegetables)

- ¼ cup toasted sunflower seeds, sesame seeds, or peanuts
- Salt to taste

Combine all the ingredients, adding salt to taste. Serve on whole-grain bread.

4. Marinated Mushrooms with Tofu Spread   Serves 4

2 tablespoons salad oil	¼ cup finely chopped celery
1 tablespoon vinegar or lemon juice	1 scallion, chopped fine
¼ teaspoon salt	1 cup tofu spread (see page 57)
¼ teaspoon dried basil leaves	Leaf lettuce
Pepper to taste	4 slices bread
¼ pound fresh mushrooms, sliced	4 thin tomato slices

Make a marinade of the oil, vinegar, salt, basil, and pepper. Add the mushrooms, celery, and scallion. Let stand for an hour or so before using.

Spread bread with ¼ cup of the tofu spread. Top with lettuce and the marinated mushrooms. Garnish with a tomato slice and serve open-faced.

GARDEN SANDWICHES WITH TOFU SAUCES

A garden sandwich is just a lot of fresh vegetables, or perhaps fruits, heaped on a slice of bread and served open-faced to be eaten with a knife and fork—Danish style. Start with a slice of bread: Use white, wheat, rye, or pumpernickel spread with butter, margarine, or mayonnaise. Add a leaf of lettuce: butter, red, green leaf, or iceberg. Now pile on the garden:

Recipes for a variety of "gardens" follow these construction details (see pages 60–62).

Top with one of a selection of sauces:

Recipes for these sauces or dressings are also given below (see pages 62–64).

Garnish with:

1. a mound of alfalfa sprouts
2. a tomato slice
3. a very thin onion slice
4. sliced raw mushrooms
5. slices of hard-cooked egg
6. a slice of cheese or grated cheese
7. anything else that comes to mind

"GARDENS" FOR GARDEN SANDWICHES

1. Carrot-Raisin

each recipe makes 4 sandwiches

½ cup mashed firm tofu
1 cup shredded carrots
¼ cup raisins

¼ cup chopped celery
1 teaspoon lemon juice
Pinch of salt

Combine all the ingredients, blending well. Pile on a slice of bread with lettuce and top with sweet sauce (see page 63) or any other sauce. Garnish as desired.

2. Tomato-Onion

3 medium-sized fresh tomatoes
2 whole green onions
½ cup chopped firm tofu
1 tablespoon chopped fresh basil, or 1 teaspoon dried basil

½ teaspoon salt
Pepper to taste

Cut the tomatoes into quarters and remove the seeds. Chop into kidney-bean-sized pieces. Slice the onions, including the green part, very thin. Combine all the ingredients and pile on bread slices that have been buttered and layered with lettuce. Top with a sauce of your choice (see pages 62–64) and any garnish. Fresh and tasty!

3. Zucchini-Radish

1 cup chopped zucchini
½ cup chopped radishes (red or white)
½ cup chopped firm tofu
1 teaspoon lemon juice

¼ cup raisins
½ teaspoon curry powder
¼ to ½ teaspoon salt
Pepper to taste

Combine all the ingredients, blending well. Heap on a slice of bread that has been buttered and topped with a leaf of lettuce. Serve with any sauce and garnish. Yogurt-garlic sauce is especially good (see page 63).

4. Creole

¼ cup chopped onion	½ cup chopped firm tofu
¼ cup chopped green pepper	¼ teaspoon dried oregano
	½ teaspoon chili powder
¼ cup chopped celery	¼ to ½ teaspoon salt
½ cup chopped tomato	Pepper to taste

Combine all the ingredients and mix lightly. Pile on prepared slices of bread and serve with a sauce of your choice.

5. Bean and Bacon

2 slices bacon, fried crisp, or 3 tablespoons bacon bits	¼ cup chopped celery
	¼ cup chopped onion
	1 tablespoon mild vinegar
1 cup cooked kidney or chili beans	¼ to ½ teaspoon salt
	¼ teaspoon pepper
½ cup chopped firm tofu	

Crumble the bacon into bits. Combine with the remaining ingredients, blending well. Prepare bread with a leaf of lettuce and pile bean mixture on top. Use a mild sauce and garnishes to taste.

6. Fruit Salad

1½ cups any fruits in season, cubed and mixed together (peaches, pears, apricots, apples, oranges, etc.)	2 teaspoons lemon juice
	½ cup mashed firm tofu
	¼ cup chopped nuts or sunflower seeds
	1 tablespoon sugar

Sprinkle the fruit with lemon juice and mix lightly with a fork. Fold in the tofu, nuts, and sugar. Spoon onto bread that has been buttered and dressed with a leaf of lettuce. Top with a sweet sauce and a sprinkle of brown sugar.

7. Sweet and Sour Rice

1 cup cooked rice
½ cup firm tofu, chopped
  to rice grain size
2 teaspoons sugar
1½ tablespoons mild vinegar

Salt and pepper to taste
¼ cup chopped sweet
  pepper (red or green)
¼ cup chopped jicama or
  water chestnuts
¼ cup chopped almonds
¼ cup raisins

Mix the rice, tofu, sugar, vinegar, salt, and pepper. Sample and correct flavor to your taste. Mix in the sweet pepper, jicama or water chestnuts, almonds, and raisins. Serve on prepared bread slices garnished with a thin slice of sweet onion.

8. Mixed Vegetables

1½ cups mixed vegetables,
  cooked or raw, cubed
  and mixed together
  (leftover peas, carrots,
  green beans, cauliflower,
  broccoli, etc.)

½ cup firm tofu, chopped
  into small bits
1 tablespoon chopped
  onion
1 tablespoon vinegar
½ teaspoon salt

Combine all the ingredients. Pile on bread and lettuce leaves and top with a sauce and a garnish or two.

SAUCES FOR GARDEN SANDWICHES

1. Honey-Spice Sauce   1 cup

½ cup soft tofu
¼ cup buttermilk, or 3
  tablespoons water plus 1
  teaspoon lemon juice

2 tablespoons honey
½ teaspoon pumpkin pie
  spice
Pinch of salt

Combine the ingredients in a blender jar and puree. Add more liquid to thin and more honey and spice to taste. Serve on Garden Sandwiches such as Carrot-Raisin (see page 60) and Fruit Salad (see page 61). Also fine on pancakes and waffles.

2. Yogurt Sweet Sauce   1 cup

½ cup soft tofu
¼ cup yogurt
1 teaspoon lemon juice

1 to 3 tablespoons sugar,
or to taste
Pinch of salt

Combine the tofu, yogurt, lemon juice, 1 tablespoon of
the sugar, and salt in a blender jar and puree. Taste and
correct flavoring, adding more sugar if necessary. Add
water to thin, if needed. Serve on fruit sandwiches.

3. Yogurt-Garlic Sauce   1 cup

½ cup soft tofu
¼ cup yogurt
¼ cup buttermilk
1 large clove garlic, or ½
teaspoon garlic powder

¼ teaspoon salt
¼ teaspoon pepper

Combine all the ingredients in a blender jar and blend
until very smooth. Taste and correct seasoning. Add water
to thin, if necessary.

4. Sesame Sauce (Tahini)   1 cup

½ cup soft tofu
¼ cup tahini (ground
sesame seeds)
1 to 2 tablespoons lemon
juice

1 clove garlic
¼ to ½ teaspoon salt
Pepper to taste

Combine tofu, tahini, 1 tablespoon of the lemon juice,
garlic, salt, and pepper in a blender jar and blend until
smooth. Add additional lemon juice and salt to correct
flavor as desired. Add water to thin, if needed.

5. Tarragon Sauce   1 cup

½ cup soft tofu
2 tablespoons salad oil
1 tablespoon Dijon
mustard
1 tablespoon lemon juice

½ teaspoon dried tarragon
½ teaspoon salt
Pepper to taste
1 to 2 tablespoons water
or buttermilk

Combine tofu, oil, mustard, lemon juice, tarragon, salt,

pepper, and water. Blend very smooth, adding more liquid for proper consistency. Taste and correct seasoning.

6. Beau Monde Sauce   1 cup

½ cup soft tofu
¼ cup soy milk, buttermilk, or yogurt
¼ teaspoon salt

⅛ teaspoon pepper
½ teaspoon beau monde seasoning
1 teaspoon lemon juice

Combine tofu, liquid, salt, pepper, seasoning, and lemon juice in the container of a blender and blend until smooth. Add water to thin. Taste and correct seasoning.

5

THE TOFUBURGER

Tofu makes the king of burgers. The basic mix can be flavored to suit any taste. The recipe is the equivalent in volume to a pound of ground meat.

TOFUBURGER MIX

2¼ cups

1 12-ounce package firm tofu (1½ cups)
¼ to ½ cup whole-wheat flour
½ to 1 teaspoon salt, or to taste

1 egg (optional)
¼ cup oil (mix will be 20 percent fat)

Mash or crumble the tofu. It should be *very* firm tofu. If it is not, press it before using it (see page 7). Add ¼ cup flour, salt, egg, and as much oil as you wish. If the mixture does not stay together, add more flour until it is about the consistency of ground meat.

This mixture can be made ahead and stored in the refrigerator for up to a week.

Use it as it is or mix it with flavors and fillers for variety. Almost any flavor or texture can be added to the mix. You can use vegetables, fruits, nuts, seeds, herbs, or spices. Add cooked grains such as rice, wheat, or barley; and/or add mashed potatoes or cooked yellow squash.

You can also add meat, fish, seafood, or cured meats such as bacon, ham, or sausage.

Shape into patties and either fry them or bake them until brown and crusty. Serve with rolls as you would ordinary hamburgers. Or serve them with a favorite sauce or gravy.

VEGETABLE TOFUBURGERS

6 to 8 patties

1 small onion
1 carrot
1 small stalk celery
2 tablespoons chopped parsley
¼ to ½ cup any other vegetables, cooked or uncooked
2 tablespoons oil
¼ to ½ cup sesame seeds, sunflower seeds, millet, or raisins, or a combination

½ teaspoon salt
Pepper to taste
½ teaspoon garlic powder (optional)
1 recipe tofuburger mix (see page 65)

Chop the onion, carrot, celery, parsley, and vegetable and sauté in the oil for a minute or two. Stir in the seeds, raisins, salt, pepper, and garlic powder. Mix with the tofuburger.

Form into patties and fry or bake. Serve on buns with the usual accoutrements such as catsup, pickles, and the like.

CHICKEN BURGERS

8 patties

1 recipe tofuburger mix
(see page 65)
1 cup diced cooked
chicken, or 1 7-ounce
can of chicken
3 teaspoons dried chicken
bouillon or dry
chicken soup mix

1 tablespoon chopped
parsley
2 tablespoons chopped
onion
Salt and pepper

Combine the tofuburger, chicken, chicken flavoring, parsley, and onion. Add salt and pepper to taste.

Form into patties, using ⅓ cup for each. Fry in a small amount of fat until very crisp, or bake in a 400°F. oven until brown and crusty, about 45 minutes.

The patties can be served in sandwiches with toppings of lettuce, tomato, mayonnaise, or relishes. They may also be served with a gravy or sauce as a main course.

TURKEY BURGERS

8 patties

1 recipe tofuburger mix
(see page 65)
1 cup diced cooked turkey
meat
1 small onion or 2 green
onions, chopped
1 tablespoon chopped
parsley

1 tablespoon tomato paste
or catsup
½ teaspoon poultry
seasoning
Salt and pepper to taste

Combine the tofuburger, turkey, onion, parsley, tomato paste, and poultry seasoning together. Season to taste with salt and pepper.

Form into patties and either fry or bake about 45 minutes

in a 400°F. oven until brown and crispy. Serve in a sandwich or as a main course. They are equally good cold.

CURRY BURGER WITH FRUIT

8 patties

1 recipe tofuburger mix (see page 65)	¼ cup raisins
½ cup chopped apple	3 tablespoons plain yogurt
¼ cup chopped onion	2 to 3 teaspoons curry powder, or to taste
1 tablespoon lemon juice	½ teaspoon salt, or to taste
½ cup mixed seeds or nuts	½ teaspoon black pepper

Combine all the ingredients, blending well. Taste and correct seasoning. Fry in oil until crisp or bake in a 400°F. oven for about 45 minutes, or until brown and crisp. Serve with a dollop of yogurt and a spoonful of chutney.

SEAFOOD CURRY BURGER

8 patties

1 recipe tofuburger mix (see page 65)	2 teaspoons curry powder, or to taste
1 tablespoon oil	½ teaspoon salt
½ cup chopped onion	½ teaspoon pepper
1 large clove garlic, chopped fine	2 tablespoons lemon juice
1 cup shrimp, crabmeat, or tuna 6½-ounce or 1 can	

Have the tofuburger mix ready. Heat the oil in a skillet and sauté the onion and garlic until the onion is transparent. Stir in the seafood, curry powder, salt, and pepper. Cook, stirring, for a minute or two until well mixed. Add this to the tofuburger mix along with the lemon juice. Taste and correct seasoning.

Form into patties and fry in oil until very crisp, or bake in a 400°F. oven about 45 minutes, until crisp and brown. These do well, too, with chutney and yogurt.

BACON AND CHEESE BURGERS

8 patties

6 slices bacon
1 small onion, chopped
1 tablespoon Worcestershire sauce
½ teaspoon pepper

1 recipe tofuburger mix (see page 65)
1 cup grated Cheddar cheese, or 8 slices American cheese

Fry the bacon until crisp and crumble. Fry the onion in the bacon fat until brown. Drain and discard fat.

Combine the bacon, onion, Worcestershire sauce, pepper, and tofuburger and form into patties. Fry in hot fat or bake in a 400°F. oven about 45 minutes until crisp and brown. When almost done, place 2 tablespoons of grated cheese or a slice of American cheese on each one and let it melt. Serve with hot rolls or toasted English muffins.

CORN AND PEPPER BURGERS

8 patties

1 recipe tofuburger mix (see page 65)
1 tablespoon oil
1 small onion, chopped
½ green or red sweet pepper, or ¼ of each, chopped

1 cup whole-kernel corn
½ teaspoon salt
½ teaspoon pepper

Have the tofuburger prepared. Heat the oil in a skillet and sauté the onion and peppers until onion is transparent but still crisp. Add the corn, salt, and pepper and cook until the water evaporates. Mix with the tofuburger.

Form into patties and fry or bake in a 400°F. oven about 45 minutes until golden brown.

BROWN ONION BURGERS

6 patties

3 to 4 large onions
3 tablespoons oil
½ teaspoon salt

1 recipe tofuburger mix
(see page 65)

Slice the onions ¼-inch thick. Heat the oil in a large skillet. Add the onions and salt and fry, stirring often, until they are very brown.

Form the tofuburger into patties and fry in another skillet until they are brown and crisp. Serve the burgers topped with a great pile of browned onions and a scoop of mashed potatoes. A plain but delicious dinner.

BLUE CHEESE BURGERS

6 patties

2 ounces blue cheese,
crumbled
2 cloves garlic, chopped
fine

1 recipe tofuburger mix
(see page 65)

Combine the ingredients, blending well. Shape into patties and fry until brown and crusty. Serve on toasted English muffins with a garnish of lettuce and tomato.

BEEF AND TOFU BURGERS

8 to 10 patties

1 tablespoon oil
1 large onion, chopped
½ pound ground beef
½ teaspoon salt

½ teaspoon pepper
1 recipe tofuburger mix
(see page 65)

Heat the oil in a skillet and sauté the onion until transparent, but still crisp. Transfer to a bowl and blend in the remaining ingredients. Shape into patties and fry in oil, or bake in a 400°F. oven about 45 minutes until brown and crisp. Serve as you would any beefburger.

CHILI BURGERS

8 patties

1 tablespoon oil
1 large onion, chopped
½ green pepper, chopped
1 tablespoon chili powder
1 tablespoon tomato sauce
or catsup
½ teaspoon salt

½ teaspoon pepper
1 recipe tofuburger mix
(see page 65)
1 1-pound can chili beans
or chili con carne, or
1½ cups homemade
chili

Heat the oil in a skillet and sauté the onion and green pepper until onion is transparent, but still crisp. Add the chili powder, tomato sauce, salt, and pepper and stir until well mixed. Add to tofuburger and stir well. Shape patties and either bake at 400°F. about 45 minutes or fry until crisp and brown.

Heat the chili. Serve the burgers with a generous helping of chili spooned over them.

CRISPY NUT AND SEED BURGERS

8 to 10 patties

1 cup mixed chopped nuts and seeds
1 tablespoon oil
1 clove garlic, chopped
2 tablespoons dried onion soup mix

1 recipe tofuburger mix (see page 65)
8 or 10 large slices of bread, crusts removed
¼ cup melted butter or oil

Preheat oven to 350°F. Sauté the nuts and seeds in the oil. Add the garlic and soup mix and stir together. Remove from heat, add the tofuburger, and mix well.

Form the mixture into 8 or 10 long cylinders, like hot dogs, and roll up in the bread slices. Fasten with toothpicks. Brush with melted butter and arrange on a baking sheet. Bake in the oven about 45 minutes until brown and crusty. Serve hot with a side dish of sauerkraut.

LAMB AND TOFU BURGERS

8 patties

1 tablespoon oil
1 large onion, chopped
½ green pepper, chopped
½ pound ground lamb
1 teaspoon dried marjoram
1 teaspoon dried thyme

1 teaspoon sugar
1 tablespoon catsup
½ teaspoon salt
½ teaspoon pepper
1 recipe tofuburger mix (see page 65)

Heat the oil in a skillet. Add the onion and pepper and cook until the onion is transparent, but still crisp. Remove from the stove. Stir in the lamb, marjoram, thyme, sugar, catsup, salt, and pepper. Cook, stirring briskly, for about 2 minutes.

Mix with the tofuburger in a bowl. Shape into patties and either fry in oil, or bake in a 400°F. oven about 45 minutes until brown and crisp. Serve with a brown sauce and steamed rice. Don't forget the mint jelly.

LAMB AND TOFU BURGERS WITH ORANGE

8 to 10 patties

1 tablespoon oil
1 large onion, chopped
½ teaspoon dried sage
1 tablespoon orange juice
1 tablespoon grated orange rind

1 tablespoon mint jelly
½ teaspoon salt
½ teaspoon pepper
½ pound ground lean lamb
1 recipe tofuburger mix (see page 65)

Heat the oil in a skillet and sauté the onion until transparent, but still crisp. Blend in the sage, orange juice and rind, jelly, salt, and pepper, mixing well. Transfer to a bowl and combine with the lamb and tofuburger.

Form into patties and fry in oil until brown and crusty. Drain on paper towels and serve hot, with chutney and yogurt, in pocket bread (pita) or on toasted English muffins.

FISH BURGERS

8 to 10 patties

½ to 1 pound any cooked fish, flaked
1 recipe tofuburger mix (see page 65)
1 egg

2 to 4 tablespoons flour (if needed)
½ teaspoon salt
½ teaspoon pepper
2 teaspoons lemon juice

Mix the fish, tofuburger, and egg together. Add flour as needed to make the mixture hold together. Blend in salt, pepper, and lemon juice to taste.

Form into patties and fry in hot oil until crisp and brown. Serve in sandwiches with tartar sauce, or as a main course with a white sauce and boiled potatoes.

SMOKY TOFUBURGER

10 patties

1 cup flaked smoked fish
(about ½ pound)
¼ cup chopped parsley
1 teaspoon prepared
mustard

1 recipe tofuburger mix
(see page 65)
¼ cup sesame seeds
Salt and pepper to taste

Combine the fish, parsley, mustard, tofuburger, and sesame seeds, mixing well. Add salt and pepper to taste.

Form into cakes or patties and fry in hot fat until brown and crisp. Serve either hot or cold.

SALMON PATTIES

12 to 15 patties

1 tablespoon oil
¼ cup chopped onion
¼ cup chopped celery
2 tablespoons chopped
parsley
2 teaspoons celery seeds
1 teaspoon paprika

1 tablespoon lemon juice
½ teaspoon salt
½ teaspoon pepper
1 recipe tofuburger mix
(see page 65)
1 (1-pound) can of salmon,
flaked

Heat the oil in a skillet and sauté the onion and celery for about 5 minutes. Stir in the parsley, celery seeds, paprika, lemon juice, salt, and pepper. Combine this with the tofuburger and salmon, mixing thoroughly. Taste and correct seasoning.

Form into patties or balls and bake in a 350°F. oven, or fry in hot fat until brown and crusty. These may be served as a sandwich on a bun with tartar sauce and garnishes, or as a main course with a lemon sauce (see page 50) and boiled potatoes.

TUNA BURGERS

10 to 12 patties

1 (6½-ounce) can of tuna
2 tablespoons dried
  chopped onion
2 tablespoons catsup

1 recipe tofuburger mix
  (see page 65)
  Salt and pepper to taste

Drain oil or water from the tuna and flake. Mix in the onion and the catsup, then mix in the tofuburger. Taste and add salt and pepper as needed.

Form into patties or cakes and bake in a 350°F. oven 30 to 45 minutes until brown. Serve hot or cold as a sandwich on a toasted English muffin with lettuce and a slice of tomato.

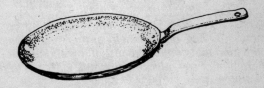

6

SOUPS

Tofu has some very special uses in soups. You can do one of three things with it.

1. *Add it as it is, either in pieces or mashed OR*
2. *Blend it with cornstarch and water and add to soups as a thickener OR*
3. *Use it in pieces and as a thickener in the same soup.*

Lots of people like creamy soups but don't want to use milk. Tofu can act as the "milk" in a creamy soup. By combining soft tofu and water you can make a milk-like mixture that works well in creamed soups.

Soy milk can also be used instead of dairy milk, but it is not as easy to find as is tofu. You can make soy milk from soybeans. It is a step on the way to making tofu (see recipe on page 18).

A word of caution: Do not boil creamed soups made with tofu. (Boiling doesn't help any creamed soup, not even the kind that comes in cans!) If this should happen, a small amount of soy milk or dairy milk will help to restore the creamy texture.

Tofu Pieces in Soups:*

1. Plain Cubes

1 or 2 slices of firm tofu

Cut into ½-inch cubes and use in soups or on salads in their natural state.

*These cubes can be used in salads, too, just as you would use croutons.

2. Marinated Cubes

2 slices firm tofu
¼ cup soy sauce
¼ cup white wine or water

½ teaspoon onion or garlic powder

Cut tofu into ½-inch cubes. Combine soy sauce, wine, and onion powder. Pour over tofu cubes and let stand for several hours. Drain and use in soups or on salads.

3. Fried or Dried Tofu Cubes

2 slices firm tofu
Soy marinade as above

Cube tofu and marinate as above. Drain the marinated tofu on paper towels. These can be fried until golden brown, or dried in a 275°F. oven, about 20 minutes or until very crisp. Store in refrigerator and use in soups or on salads.

4. Clam or Fish Flavored Tofu Cubes

2 slices firm tofu
1 cup clam juice or fish stock

Cut the tofu into ½-inch cubes. Boil the clam juice or fish stock until reduced by half. Marinate the tofu cubes for the stock for several hours or overnight. Drain and use in salads or soups.

CREAM OF EGGPLANT SOUP

Serves 6

3 tablespoons butter or margarine

3 medium-sized onions, chopped

1½ cups chopped celery

1 large eggplant, diced

3 medium-sized potatoes, diced

2 teaspoons curry powder

½ teaspoon each dried sweet basil, dried thyme, and pepper

1 teaspoon salt

1 large clove garlic, mashed

4 cups chicken stock

1 cup soy milk or dairy milk

1 cup water

2 tablespoons cornstarch or flour

1 cup soft tofu

2 (½-inch) slices firm tofu, diced

Yogurt

Melt the butter in a large pot, add the onion and celery and cook, stirring, for a minute or two over medium heat. The eggplant and potatoes can be peeled or unpeeled, as you choose. Stir the eggplant and potatoes into the onion-celery mixture. Sauté the vegetables for about 10 minutes, stirring frequently.

Add the curry powder, basil, thyme, pepper, salt, and garlic, mixing well. Cook 5 minutes longer and then add the chicken stock. Simmer about 5 minutes more until the vegetables are done.

Combine the milk, water, cornstarch and soft tofu in a blender jar and blend until very smooth. Stir into the soup and continue stirring until the soup thickens. *Do not boil.* Serve at once with firm tofu cubes and dollops of yogurt.

CREAMY POTATO SOUP

This is a basic soup that can be varied in lots of ways. Try it as is and then try a variation or two—and then design your own variations.

Serves 6 to 8

3 tablespoons butter or margarine
1 large onion, chopped
¼ cup chopped parsley
1 cup chopped celery
4 to 5 peeled potatoes, cut up (about 4 cups)
½ teaspoon salt, or to taste

¼ to ½ teaspoon pepper
4 cups chicken or beef stock
1½ cups soft tofu plus 2½ cups water or 4 cups soy milk
2 tablespoons cornstarch

Melt the butter in a large, heavy-bottomed pot and sauté the onion, parsley, and celery until the onion is limp. Add the potatoes, salt, pepper, and stock. Cover and cook until the potatoes are tender, about 20 minutes.

Combine the tofu, water, and cornstarch in a blender jar or food processor bowl and puree until smooth. Stir into the soup and cook, stirring, until slightly thickened.

If you are using soy milk instead of tofu, mix 1 cup of milk with the cornstarch. Add this to the soup and stir well. Cook until it thickens. Then add the rest of the soy milk and cook until very hot. Serve with a heavy, dark bread and a green salad for a full meal.

The soup can be served with the vegetables in chunks or it can be pureed in the blender. Serve with a garnish of fresh parsley. It can also be served cold, in which case it might be called "vichysoisse." Try these variations:

1. **Potato Mushroom Soup**

1 tablespoon butter or margarine
½ pound mushrooms, sliced

1 recipe creamy potato soup (see above)

Melt the butter and stir in the mushrooms. Cover and cook over low to medium heat for 3 minutes. Add to the basic soup, either pureed or not, and serve very hot.

2. Shrimp, Crab, Lobster, or Fish Soup

1 to 1¼ pounds cooked
seafood or fish

1 recipe creamy potato
soup (see page 79)

Add seafood or fish to basic soup just before serving.
Cook only until seafood is heated through. Serve at once.

3. Cooked Vegetable Soup

1 recipe creamy potato
soup (see page 79)

2 to 4 cups diced cooked
vegetables

Puree the basic soup and stir in the vegetables. Heat and
serve. This is an excellent way to use leftover vegetables.

LAMB AND YOGURT SOUP

Serves 6 to 8

½ cup pearl barley
2 cups water
1¼ teaspoons salt
2 tablespoons oil
1 large onion, chopped
½ pound ground lamb
½ teaspoon pepper
½ teaspoon dried oregano

½ teaspoon garlic powder
2 tablespoons dried mint
1 tablespoon flour
1 cup yogurt
1 cup soft tofu
2 cups clear soup stock
(any kind)

Combine the barley, water, and ¼ teaspoon of the salt.
Cook until barley is tender, about 1 hour.

Heat the oil in a large, heavy-bottomed pot and sauté
the onion until limp. Add the lamb and cook until the
meat is brown. Stir in the remaining 1 teaspoon salt,
pepper, oregano, garlic powder, mint, and flour. Cook for
2 or 3 minutes.

Combine the yogurt, tofu, and 1 cup of the stock in a
blender and blend until smooth. Add to the soup pot. Mix
the remaining cup of stock with the cooked barley and
add to the pot. Cook, stirring, over medium heat. Bring to
a simmer and serve at once. Garnish each bowl with a
fresh mint leaf and a slice of lemon.

COLD CUCUMBER SOUP

Serves 6

4 tablespoons butter or margarine	1 large potato, peeled and chopped
2 medium-sized onions, chopped	4 cups chicken broth
2 small cucumbers or 1 English-style cucumber, chopped	1 tablespoon cornstarch
	1 cup soft tofu
	Salt and pepper to taste

Melt the butter in a large soup pot. Add the onion and sauté for about 5 minutes, or until limp. Add the cucumbers, potato and 3 cups of the broth. Simmer until the vegetables are very soft.

Combine the remaining cup of stock with the cornstarch and tofu in a blender or food processor. Blend until very smooth. Add a cup or two of the cooked soup and blend until smooth again. Pour this mixture into a container. Blend the rest of the cooked soup in batches and add to the container. Mix well and taste before adding salt and pepper. Chill for several hours or overnight before serving.

Serve with a spoonful of yogurt or sour cream and a garnish of chopped chives or chopped dill and a slice of lemon.

7
TOFU FOR DINNER

Dinners have to take second place on my personal list of favorite tofu dishes. That's because I am a dessert person. If you are a main course person, you will be delighted with these recipes.

Dinner is a most natural time for tofu to be served. It has been a part of Chinese and Japanese meals for centuries, but in very different ways than you will find here. Where the Oriental cuisines use tofu only as a separate food, these recipes use tofu both as a food and an ingredient.

You will find recipes here for American-style and ethnic-style preparations that use tofu in both ways. When used in its natural form, tofu can be sliced or cut into chunks and used in much the same way as meat. When used as an ingredient, tofu is mashed or blended with other ingredients and used in an array of dishes, from quiche to meat loaf.

"Meat and potatoes" people will be won over with any one of these recipes.

BAKED, BROILED, BARBECUED, AND FRIED

Firm tofu can be used as is in dozens of ways. It can be diced, sliced, or cubed. Then it can be baked, broiled, pan-fried, deep fried, or skewered and barbecued. It is especially good when marinated and then cooked. Almost any marinade will work.

The tofu must be firm or it cannot be prepared in these ways. The difference between firm and soft tofu is that the latter has more water content. To make firm tofu from soft

*tofu you need only press out the excess water until the
desired consistency is achieved. The method for pressing
tofu is on page 7.*

MARINADES FOR FIRM TOFU

1. Honey-Soy Marinade

¼ cup soy sauce
¼ cup oil
¼ cup dry wine, red or
    white
1 clove garlic
1 tablespoon lemon juice
2 tablespoons honey

½ teaspoon ground ginger,
    or 1 1-inch piece fresh
    ginger
¼ cup water
½ teaspoon toasted sesame
    oil (optional)

Combine all the ingredients in a blender jar and blend
until smooth and light in color.

2. Lemon-Garlic

¼ cup oil
¼ lemon, unpeeled
¼ cup water
¼ small onion
1 clove garlic

½ teaspoon mace
¼ teaspoon ground cloves
¼ teaspoon salt
¼ teaspoon pepper

Combine all the ingredients in a blender and blend until
liquefied.

3. Soy

⅓ cup soy sauce
⅓ cup water

¼ cup oil

Blend the soy sauce, water, and oil together.

4. Orange-Marmalade

¼ cup orange marmalade
¼ cup very hot water

¼ cup soy sauce
¼ cup white wine or water

Combine the marmalade with the hot water and stir until
it dissolves. Add the soy sauce and the wine.

BAKED TOFU

8 (½-inch) slices of firm tofu

Marinate the tofu slices for 1 hour or more, turning frequently. Arrange the slices on a greased baking sheet and bake at 350°F. until done. Baking will take from 1 to 2 hours. A long baking time makes the tofu dry and chewy; a short baking time and the tofu will be soft and more custard-like.

Make a sauce of the leftover marinade:

5 teaspoons cornstarch   1 cup marinade
½ cup cold water

Dissolve the cornstarch in the cold water. Add the marinade and heat until the sauce thickens. Serve with baked slices.

These baked tofu slices are excellent eaten cold for lunch or for a snack. Split them and use them instead of bread for sandwiches. Make a pocket in them and stuff them. Cut them in cubes and use them in other tofu dishes.

You may have seen baked slices at your grocery store. They come in vacuum packages and are very expensive, as are most precooked foods. Now you can make them yourself at a fraction of the cost.

BROILED TOFU

8 (½-inch) slices firm tofu

Marinate the slices for 1 hour or more. (You can also broil the slices without marinating.) Place the slices on the broiler rack and broil as you would a steak. Watch them carefully as they will brown very rapidly. They will puff up and be crusty on the outside and soft and creamy on the inside.

Serve the broiled slices with a sauce of your choice or one on pages 46–52.

FRIED TOFU

8 (½-inch) slices of firm tofu
cut in cubes or triangles (any size)

The tofu can be pan-fried or deep fried. Be sure to drain marinated tofu on paper towels before frying to prevent fat spattering.

Fry at high heat until crisp and brown. Drain on paper towels. The fried tofu can be served immediately or set aside and reheated later to serve with sauces or in other dishes.

You can serve fried tofu with the sauce on p. 84 accompanied by rice and a vegetable, for a full, rich main dish.

The Orange-Marmalade marinade (see page 83) can be used as the basis for another delicious sauce:

Sweet and Sour Sauce

2 tablespoons cornstarch
½ cup pineapple juice
1 cup Orange Marmalade
 marinade

¼ cup vinegar
2 tablespoons brown sugar
2 tablespoons catsup
1 tablespoon soy sauce

Dissolve the cornstarch in the pineapple juice and combine with the marinade, vinegar, sugar, and catsup. Heat until the sauce thickens. Taste and add soy sauce as needed. Thin with water or additional pineapple juice. Serve with fried tofu and boiled rice.

To carry this recipe to its logical conclusion as a relative of the well-known Chinese Sweet and Sour Pork, try this:

Sweet and Sour Tofu

1 medium-sized onion, cut into wedges	1 tablespoon oil
1 medium-sized green pepper, cut into bite-sized pieces	½ cup sliced mushrooms
	½ cup pineapple chunks
Other hard vegetables such as carrots, broccoli, celery, etc., cut into bite-sized pieces	⅛ pound fresh bean sprouts
	1 recipe Sweet and Sour sauce (see page 85)
	1 (12-ounce) package firm tofu, cubed and fried

In a wok or large skillet stir-fry the hard vegetables in the oil. Cover and let steam until they are cooked to your liking. Stir in the mushrooms, and cook for 1 minute. Stir in the pineapple and bean sprouts, and then stir in the sauce and tofu. Serve at once with boiled rice.

Chinese-Style White Rice

1 cup long-grain white rice

Wash the rice until the water runs clear. Cover the rice with water, let it stand for a few moments, and then rinse in a strainer. Repeat several times.

Place the rice in a heavy-bottomed pot and cover with water to one inch above the rice. Heat to boiling, cover, and reduce heat to very low. Steam in the covered pot until rice is cooked but not too soft, about 10 to 15 minutes. (If the grains show two points at each end, the rice is overcooked, but never mind, next time you will know better.)

Remove the cover from the pot and leave rice over very low heat until ready to served.

BARBECUED TOFU

1-inch cubes of firm tofu (4 to 6 per serving)

Any marinade from page 83 (optional)
   Your choice of:
   Onion wedges
   Tomato wedges
   Whole mushrooms
   Fresh or canned pineapple chunks
   Cantaloupe cubes
   Eggplant cubes (marinate with tofu)
   Lemon slices
   Orange wedges, with rind
   Banana slices
   Green pepper or sweet red pepper
Use the above in any combination and in any order. Skewer alternately with tofu cubes, marinated or plain, and barbecue over coals or bake in a 400°F. oven. Baste with the marinade. Cook, turning frequently, until the tofu and vegetables and fruits are done to your liking, about 15 minutes.
Serve on a bed of rice with the sauce on p. 84.

QUICHE

A quiche is a pie that is served as the main course for luncheon or dinner. It is filled with lots of good things such as cheese, vegetables, meats, fish, bacon and so on. Then these good things are held together with a custard, traditionally made with lots of eggs and milk.

A quiche can be made with tofu instead of eggs and without any milk at all. This makes it possible for people on low cholesterol diets to eat quiche after all.

Here is the method for making quiche step by step:

Step 1: Make a pie crust or crumb crust, for a 9-inch pie (see page 157)

If you use a pastry crust it must be partially baked before filling. Bake the shell in a preheated 400°F. oven for 7 minutes. A crumb shell must be completely baked.

Step 2: Make the basic tofu quiche mix

1 cup water, soy milk, or milk
1 tablespoon cornstarch
1 cup soft tofu
2 tablespoons melted butter or oil
¼ cup grated Parmesan, Romano or other strong cheese

½ teaspoon salt
1 teaspoon lemon juice
1 teaspoon Worcestershire sauce
Pepper to taste
1 or 2 eggs (optional)

Combine all the ingredients in a blender and blend until smooth. It should be the consistency of thick cream.

Step 3: Set the quiche mix aside while preparing the other part of the filling.

1. Onion Quiche

4 cups chopped onion
2 tablespoons oil
½ teaspoon salt
Pepper to taste
1 8- or 9-inch prepared pie shell (see page 157)

1 recipe tofu quiche mix (see above)
Grated cheese and butter for topping

Preheat the oven to 350°F. Sauté the onion in the oil, stirring until fully cooked but not browned. The liquid should be entirely evaporated. Add salt and pepper to taste. Spread in the pie shell and pour in the tofu quiche mix. Sprinkle with cheese and dot with butter. Bake for about 25 to 30 minutes, or until center is firm. Cool for at least 5 minutes before serving.

Follow the three-step method with the following fillings:

2. Mushroom Quiche

2 tablespoons butter or oil
2 to 3 cups sliced raw
  mushrooms
¼ teaspoon dried basil
½ teaspoon salt
1 tablespoon dried
  chopped onion

1 recipe tofu quiche mix
  (see page 88)
1 cup shredded Swiss
  cheese
1 8- or 9-inch prepared
  pie shell (see page 157)

Preheat the oven to 350°F. Heat the butter in a skillet and sauté the mushrooms for 3 minutes, stirring constantly. Add the basil, salt, and onion. Cool for about 5 minutes, then drain off any liquid. Mix the liquid with the tofu quiche mix.

Spread the mushrooms in the pie shell. Sprinkle with the cheese. Pour the quiche mix over the mushrooms and cheese. Bake for about 30 minutes, or until the pie begins to puff and the center is firm. Cool for 5 minutes before serving.

3. Bacon, Ham or Seafood Quiche

1 large onion, chopped
1 tablespoon oil
1 cup diced ham, shrimp,
  or other seafood, or ½
  cup crisp bacon pieces
½ teaspoon dried tarragon

⅔ cup grated Swiss or Jack
  cheese
1 recipe tofu quiche mix
  (see page 88)
1 8- or 9-inch prepared
  pie shell (see page 157)

Preheat the oven to 350°F. Sauté the onion in the oil until limp. Remove from the heat and add the meat or seafood and the tarragon. Mix with the cheese and tofu quiche mix and pour into the pie shell. Bake for about 30 minutes or until it begins to puff and the center is firm. Cool for 5 minutes before serving.

4. Vegetable Quiche

1 medium-sized onion	Pinch of nutmeg
1 small green pepper	½ teaspoon salt
1 stalk celery	1 cup grated Cheddar
1 large carrot	cheese
1 small zucchini	1 recipe tofu quiche mix
2 tablespoons oil	(see page 88)
¼ teaspoon dried thyme	1 8- or 9-inch prepared
¼ teaspoon dried marjoram	pie crust (see page 157)

Preheat the oven to 350°F. Chop the onion, green pepper, celery, carrot, and zucchini and sauté in the oil until partially cooked. Blend in the thyme, marjoram, nutmeg, and salt and cook 1 minute longer. Combine with the cheese and the tofu mix. Pour into the pie shell and bake for about 30 minutes, or until it begins to puff and the center is firm. Cool 5 minutes before serving.

5. Spinach Quiche

1 10-ounce package frozen chopped spinach	1 clove garlic, chopped
	1 recipe tofu quiche mix (see page 88)
1 medium-sized onion, chopped	¼ cup grated Cheddar cheese
2 tablespoons oil	1 8-inch or 9-inch pie
2 tablespoons chopped parsley	shell (see page 157)

Preheat the oven to 350°F. Cook and drain the spinach according to package directions. Sauté the onion in the oil until it is transparent. Add the parsley, garlic, and spinach and stir to blend. Mix vegetables with the tofu quiche mix and half of the grated cheese. Pour into the pie shell. Sprinkle the rest of the cheese on the top.

Bake for about 25 minutes, or until it begins to puff and is firm in the center. Cool 5 minutes before serving.

TOFU FILLINGS

It is becoming increasingly popular to make "filled" foods. Sometimes the names of the preparations are unfamiliar, but they use familiar ingredients and are easy to make. Tofu makes an excellent "filling" or "stuffing" not only for the well-known "crepe," but for such things as cannelloni, empanadas, pasties, knishes, blintzes, tiropeta and others.

The recipe below is for a tofu filling mix that will be used as the basis for the recipes that follow:

TOFU FILLING MIX

2½ cups

2 cups mashed soft tofu
¼ cup flour

½ teaspoon salt
1 egg, beaten (optional)

Blend the tofu, flour, and salt together by hand or with a beater. The tofu should not be very watery; if it is, press it for a few minutes (see instructions on page 7). Stir in the egg. (The egg is for lightness and is not essential.)

ITALIAN-STYLE FILLINGS

Lasagna, cannelloni, manicotti, and conchigli are some of the Italian preparations that call for fillings. Lasagna is perhaps the most familiar. It is made with broad noodles that are layered in a baking pan. Cannelloni can be made with a pancake about 6 inches in diameter that is filled and rolled. Manicotti is a very large macaroni that is designed to be filled. Conchiglie are very large shell macaroni, also made to be filled.

All of these pastas, or noodles, are precooked, filled, arranged in a baking dish, topped with sauces, garnished with cheese, and baked until bubbly and browned. Serve them as a main course accompanied by crusty Italian bread and a green salad, and perhaps a red wine.

1. Spinach Filling   4½ cups

2 10-ounce packages
  frozen chopped spinach
1 recipe tofu filling mix
  (see page 91)
½ cup grated
  Parmesan-type cheese
2 tablespoons chopped
  parsley

½ teaspoon dried oregano
  Pinch of nutmeg
½ teaspoon salt
  Pepper to taste
1 large clove garlic,
  chopped, or ¼ teaspoon
  garlic powder

Cook the spinach according to package directions. Drain
thoroughly and chop. You should have 1½ cups of spinach. Combine the spinach with the remaining ingredients.
Taste and correct the seasoning.

2. Cheese Filling   2 cups

1¼ cups tofu filling mix (see
  page 91 ½ recipe)
½ cup grated Parmesan or
  Romano cheese
½ teaspoon dried oregano

1 clove garlic, chopped
  fine, or ¼ teaspoon
  garlic powder
¼ teaspoon salt
  Pepper to taste

Combine all the ingredients. Taste and correct seasoning.

3. Vegetable Filling   3 cups

1½ cups chopped raw or
  cooked vegetables
  (onions, garlic, carrots,
  green pepper, celery,
  zucchini, etc., in any
  proportion)
1 tablespoon oil

1¼ cups tofu filling mix (see
  page 91)
¼ cup grated Parmesan
  cheese
½ teaspoon dried basil
  Pinch of nutmeg
½ teaspoon salt
  Pepper to taste

Sauté the raw vegetables to taste, either crisp or quite soft.
Combine with the remaining ingredients. Taste and correct seasoning.

4. Meat, Fish, or . . .   **2 to 2½ cups**

½ to 1 cup diced and   ¼ teaspoon dried oregano
  cooked meat, fish,   1 tablespoon chopped
  poultry, or sausage   parsley
1¼ cups tofu filling mix (see ½ teaspoon salt
  page 91)   Pepper to taste
1 tablespoon chopped dry
  onion

Combine all the ingredients. Taste and correct seasoning.

The methods for making the Italian-style filled main
dishes follow. Use any filling you wish.

LASAGNA

Serves 8

¼ to ½ cup bread crumbs   1 recipe Italian-style tofu
1 cup grated Parmesan   filling (see pages 92, 93)
  cheese   1 cup cubed or grated
1 recipe tomato sauce (see   mozzarella
  page 119)   Salt and pepper to taste
1 1-pound package   ⅛ pound butter or
  lasagna noodles,   margarine for top
  cooked according to
  package directions

Preheat oven to 350°F. Grease a 9- by 13-inch baking pan,
or one of equivalent size, and sprinkle with about ¼ cup
breadcrumbs and 1-2 tablespoons Parmesan cheese. Pour
in about ½ cup of tomato sauce. Cover sauce with a layer
of lasagna noodles. Spoon in tofu filling in clumps. Add
more sauce, some of the mozzarella, a sprinkling of bread
crumbs, and salt and pepper. Add another layer of noodles and repeat the process until all noodles have been
used (the top layer should be noodles). Sprinkle top with
the remaining Parmesan cheese, some salt and pepper,
and dot with butter. Bake about 35 minutes, or until
bubbly and browned. Serve with crisp bread and a green
salad.

MANICOTTI

Serves 8

1 1-pound package
  manicotti, cooked
  according to package
  directions
1 recipe Italian-style tofu
  filling (see pages 92, 93)

1 recipe tomato sauce (see
  page 119)
½ cup grated Parmesan
  cheese
3 tablespoons butter or
  margarine for top

Preheat oven to 350°F. Fill each cooked manicotti with tofu filling and arrange in a 9- by 13-inch baking dish. Top with tomato sauce. Sprinkle with cheese and dot with butter. Bake about 35 minutes, or until bubbly and browned.

CONCHIGLI

Serves 6 to 8

Preheat oven to 350°F. Conchigli is very much the same as manicotti and is made in the same way. The difference is in the shape of the pasta. Conchigli are large shells. Fill conchigli with a filling of your choice and treat them the same as the manicotti. Fill, sauce, garnish with grated cheese and bake until bubbly and browned.

CANNELLONI

Serves 6 to 8

12 to 18 6-inch crepes (see
   page 104)
1 recipe any Italian-style
  tofu filling (see pages 92, 93)
1 cup White Sauce (see
  page 50)

1 recipe tomato sauce (see
  page 119)
½ cup grated Parmesan
  cheese
3 tablespoons butter or
  margarine for top

Preheat oven to 350°F. Prepare and cook the crepes. Place about 3 tablespoons of filling on each crepe and roll into a cylinder. Arrange in a greased 9- by 13-inch baking dish, or any appropriate size. Cover crepes with white sauce, then top with tomato sauce. Sprinkle with cheese and dot with butter. Bake about 45 minutes, or until bubbly and browned. Serve with a green salad and warm Italian or French bread.

LATIN AMERICAN-STYLE FILLINGS

Enchiladas, empanadas, chimechangas, and chili relleños are some Latin American preparations that are filled. Enchiladas are rolled and filled flat corn bread rounds known as tortillas. Empanadas are pastry rounds, filled and baked. Chimechangas are wheat-flour tortillas that are filled, closed, and then deep fried. Chili relleños are long, green, chili peppers, either sweet or hot, that are filled and fried.

Choose one of following fillings to use in these dishes.

1. Cheese and Chili Filling　　　　　　　**2-plus cups**

1¼ cups tofu filling mix (see page 91)

1 cup cottage cheese

¼ to ½ cup chopped green chilies or chopped green pepper

¼ teaspoon salt, or to taste

Combine all the ingredients. Taste and correct seasoning.

2. Mushroom-Onion-Olive Filling　　　　　**2½ cups**

1 large onion, chopped

1 tablespoon oil

¼ pound fresh mushrooms, chopped

1 2-ounce to 4-ounce can chopped olives, drained

¼ cup raisins

2 teaspoons chili powder

¼ teaspoon ground allspice

1¼ cup tofu filling mix (see page 91)

Salt and pepper to taste

Sauté the onion in the oil for 2 to 3 minutes. Stir in the mushrooms and cook another 2 minutes. Remove from the heat and add the remaining ingredients.

3. Bean and Cheese Filling   3½ cups

1 large onion, chopped
1 medium-sized green
   pepper, chopped
1 tablespoon oil
1 cup mashed, cooked red
   beans or refried beans
½ cup shredded sharp
   Cheddar cheese

1 cup tofu filling mix (see
   page 91)
2 teaspoons chili powder
1 tablespoon vinegar
½ teaspoon salt, or to taste
   Pepper to taste

Sauté the onion and green pepper in the oil until limp. Mix with the beans in a bowl. Add the remaining ingredients.

The methods for making the Latin-style filled main dishes follow. Use any filling you wish.

ENCHILADAS

Serves 6

1 dozen corn tortillas
2 to 3 cups Latin-style tofu
   filling (see pages 95, 96)
1 10-ounce can tomato
   soup

2 teaspoons chili powder
1 12-ounce can whole-
   kernel corn, drained
1 cup shredded Cheddar
   cheese

Preheat oven to 250°F. Soften the tortillas by wrapping them in a damp dish towel and placing them in the oven to steam.

Spoon about ¼ cup of the filling on each tortilla, roll it up and arrange in a greased baking dish.

Dilute the soup with 1 can of water and mix with the chili powder. Pour this over the tortillas. Spread the corn over the top and sprinkle with the shredded cheese.

Increase oven temperature to 350°F. and bake for about 1 hour.

EMPENDAS

Serves 6

Pastry for double crust
pie (see page 157)
2 to 3 cups Latin American-
style tofu filling (see
pages 95, 96)

Melted butter

Preheat oven to 350°F. Divide the pastry into 12 equal portions. Roll each into a round, about ⅛ inch thick. Place 2 to 4 tablespoonfuls of filling on each round. Fold in half and seal the edges by pinching or pressing with the tines of a fork. Make little slits in the top and brush with melted butter. Bake 15 to 20 minutes until the pastry is nicely browned. Serve hot or cold.

· CHIMECHANGA

Serves 12

2 to 3 cups Latin American-
style tofu filling (see
pages 95, 96)
1 dozen wheat-flour
tortillas or ⅛-inch thick
crepes (see page 104)
Fat for deep frying or
melted butter

Shredded lettuce
Grated Cheddar cheese
Chopped or sliced fresh
tomatoes
Sour cream

Preheat oven to 350°F. Place ¼ to ⅓ cup of filling on each tortilla. Fold the sides over the filling and roll into a tight bundle. Secure with wooden toothpicks. Fry in heated oil in a deep fryer or arrange in a baking sheet and brush liberally with melted butter. Bake until crisp and brown. Serve hot on a bed or lettuce with garnishes of cheese, tomatoes, and sour cream.

CHILI RELLEÑOS

12 chilies

12 long green chilies, sweet or hot (canned chilies are available in some areas)

2 to 3 cups Latin American-style tofu filling (see pages 95, 96)

Batter: 3 eggs, separated
3 tablespoons flour
1 tablespoon water
¼ teaspoon salt

Oil for frying

1 10-ounce can tomato soup

2 teaspoons chili powder

1 cup grated Cheddar cheese (optional)

Preheat oven to 350°F. Roast the peppers until they are very brown and the skin comes away easily. Peel and remove the seeds. Fill each pepper to within ½ inch of the top.

Make a batter by beating the egg yolks, flour, water and salt together. Beat the whites until very stiff. Fold into yolk mixture. Coat stuffed peppers with the batter and fry in heated oil until brown. Arrange in a baking dish.

Combine the soup with water as directed on the can and add the chili powder. Heat to a simmer. Pour over the stuffed chilies and serve at once. If you are using the cheese, place under the broiler for just a minute or two, to melt the cheese and then serve at once.

GREEK-STYLE FILLINGS

Dolmadakia, papoutsakia, tiropeta, and spanakopeta are a few Greek possibilities for filling. Dolmadakia are filled and rolled grape leaves. Papoutsakia is scooped out and filled zucchini squash. Tiropeta is a kind of unsweetened cheese pie made with very thin sheets of pastry called filo leaves, which are the same as strudel leaves. Spanakopeta is fashioned in the same way as tiropeta, but has a spinach filling.

The first recipe below can be used for filling grape leaves and zucchini.

RICE AND RAISIN FILLING

Serves 6

1¼ cups tofu filling mix (see page 91)
½ cup uncooked rice
¼ cup oil
½ cup raisins
½ cup slivered almonds

1 teaspoon dried oregano
½ teaspoon ground cinnamon
½ teaspoon salt
½ pound ground lamb (optional)

Combine all the ingredients and mix well.

DOLMADAKIA

Serves 6

1 8-ounce jar grape leaves
1 recipe rice and raisin tofu filling (see above)
2 lemons, unpeeled and cut in wedges

8 to 10 large cloves garlic, peeled
4 tablespoons dried mint
1 teaspoon salt

Separate and wash the grape leaves and cut off the short stem with a knife or a scissors. Place about 1 tablespoon of filling on each leaf. Fold the side of the leaf over the filling and roll into 2-inch oblongs, being careful to seal each one. Arrange the filled leaves in a heavy-bottomed pot or Dutch oven. Add the lemon, garlic, mint, and salt and cover with water. Place a plate that is slightly smaller than the pot over the stuffed vine leaves to weight them down while they cook. Cover the pot.

Cook on top of the stove over low heat for 2 or 3 hours. Remove the stuffed leaves to a platter with a slotted spoon. Strain the cooking liquid and use for the following:

Sauce

¼ cup butter or margarine   Milk or cream to thin
¼ cup flour   Salt to taste
    Cooking liquid from the
    grape leaves

Melt the butter and stir in the flour. Add the cooking liquid, stirring with a whisk to prevent lumps. Thin with milk or cream, if necessary. Taste and correct seasoning.

Serve grape leaves sauced or with the sauce in a separate bowl.

This preparation is even better when left a day before serving. Cool the leaves to room temperature and refrigerate in the cooking pot. Reheat and make the sauce just before serving.

Dolmadakia are also excellent served cold or at room temperature as an appetizer. If served in this way, the cooking liquid is not thickened; a little of the thin liquid is spooned over the vine leaves before serving.

PAPOUTSAKIA

Serves 6

12 fresh zucchini, 5 to 6   8 to 10 large cloves garlic,
   inches long   peeled
 1 recipe rice and raisin   4 tablespoons dried mint
   tofu filling (see page   1 teaspoon salt
   99)
 2 lemons, unpeeled and
   cut into wedges

Wash the zucchini, cut off the stems, and scoop out as much of the flesh as you can. Stuff the squash with the tofu filling. Arrange in a heavy-bottomed pot or Dutch oven. Add the lemon, garlic, mint, salt, and enough water to just cover the squash. Weight with a plate, cover, and cook on top of the stove over low heat for 2 to 3 hours. Transfer the squash to a platter with a slotted spoon and make a sauce of the cooking liquid as in the recipe for Dolmadakia on page 99.

CHEESE AND SPINACH FILLINGS

Cheese Filling for Tiropeta   **2½ cups**

2 eggs
1¼ cups tofu filling mix (see page 91)
½ cup grated Parmesan or Kasseri cheese
¼ cup grated Swiss or Monterey Jack cheese
¼ cup melted butter

Beat the eggs until very light. Add the tofu and then the cheeses. Slowly beat in the melted butter. Fill filo leaves or puff pastry as directed on page 102.

Spinach Filling for Spanakopeta   **3½ cups**

1 10-ounce package frozen chopped spinach
½ cup minced scallions
¼ cup chopped parsley
1¼ cups tofu filling mix (see page 91)
½ cup grated Parmesan, Kasseri, or Mizithra cheese
2 eggs
Salt and pepper to taste

Cook the spinach and drain thoroughly. Mix with the scallions, parsley, tofu mix, and cheese. Beat the eggs until light and fold into the tofu mixture. Fill filo leaves as directed on page 102.

TIROPETA AND SPANAKOPETA

Serves 6 to 8

1 1-pound package of filo
   leaves
½ cup melted butter

1 recipe cheese or spinach
   filling (see page 101)

Preheat oven to 350°F. Choose a pan for baking the pastries. A round pie pan, about 9 inches in diameter or an 8- by 8-inch square pan is recommended. Grease the pan.

Separate the filo leaves and place them in the pan one or two at a time. Working quickly so they will not dry out, spread melted butter between the layers with a pastry brush. Use about half the leaves for this first layer.

Pour the filling over the bottom layer of leaves. Finish with the second half of the filo leaves, buttering as you go, a leaf or two at a time.

Bake for about 45 minutes. Serve hot as an appetizer or main course.

PANCAKE AND PASTRY FILLINGS

The most familiar filled pastry, is, of course, the familiar American pie. There are some others, notably the pastie from Cornwall, the Jewish knish, and the Russian piroshki. These and more can be made with tofu filling.

1. Potato and Onion Filling   3 cups

2 tablespoons oil
1 large onion, chopped
1 large potato 8 ounces,
   finely diced or grated
1¼ cups tofu filling mix (see
   page 91)
½ to 1 teaspoon celery
   seeds or caraway
   seeds

¼ teaspoon salt
   Pepper to taste
¼ to ½ cup chopped,
   cooked meat (optional)

Heat the oil in a skillet and sauté the onion and potato slowly until done. Remove from heat and add the remaining ingredients.

2. Mashed Potato Filling   3 cups

½ cup minced onion
3 tablespoons oil or butter
1 cup mashed potatoes
1¼ cups tofu filling mix (see page 91)

½ teaspoon salt
Pepper to taste

Sauté the onion in the oil until slightly brown. Remove from heat and blend in the remaining ingredients.

3. Fish or Seafood Filling   2½ to 3 cups

1 small onion, chopped
⅓ cup chopped celery
1 tablespoon oil
¼ pound shrimp, crabmeat, or any fish
1 tablespoon chopped parsley
¼ teaspoon garlic powder

1 teaspoon paprika
¼ teaspoon dried tarragon
½ teaspoon salt, or to taste
Pepper to taste
1¼ cups tofu filling mix (see page 91)
1 to 2 tablespoons sherry

Sauté the onion and celery in the oil until they are soft but not browned. Stir in the seafood, cooked or uncooked. Add the parsley, garlic, paprika, tarragon, salt, and pepper. Cook, stirring, for another 2 minutes. Remove from the heat and blend in the tofu and sherry.

4. Cheese Filling   2 cups

1¼ cups tofu filling mix (see page 91)
¾ cup cottage cheese, ricotta, or pot cheese
1 tablespoon lemon juice

Salt to taste
1 egg (optional)
Milk or buttermilk, to thin

In a blender or a food processor, blend the tofu, cheese, lemon juice, salt, and egg until very smooth. Add drops of milk to thin.

5. Sweet Cheese Filling   2 cups

- 1 cup tofu filling mix (see page 91)
- ¾ cup cottage cheese, ricotta, or pot cheese
- 2 to 3 tablespoons sugar, or to taste
- 2 teaspoons lemon juice
- 1 teaspoon vanilla
- Pinch *each* salt and cinnamon
- Milk to thin

Combine all the ingredients and blend until smooth. Thin with milk, if needed.

CREPES

The recipe that follows can be used for pancakes, crepes, or blintzes and the fillings can be varied as you wish.

These pancakes, when used as a main dish, can be filled and refrigerated until serving time. Reheat and top with any of the variety of sauces on pages 45 to 52.

The difference in most pancakes is one of size, rather than ingredients. Pancakes for blintzes should be about 9 inches in diameter, while dessert crepes can be as small as you like.

These pancakes must be made with eggs, which hold the batter together.

BATTER FOR THIN PANCAKES

24 (6-inch) pancakes

- 1 cup soy milk or dairy milk
- 1 cup water
- ¼ cup tofu
- 2 eggs
- ¼ cup oil or melted butter
- ¼ teaspoon salt
- 1 cup flour
  (1 tablespoon sugar for sweet crepes)

Combine all the ingredients in a blender and blend until very smooth. Refrigerate for an hour before using. The batter should be the consistency of heavy cream. Add water to thin, or more flour to thicken.

Fry the crepes in a lightly greased 6, 7, 8, or 9-inch skillet. Pour ⅛ to ¼ cup of the batter into the heated pan and roll it around until it covers the bottom. Cook until the top is dry. Crepes for filling do not need to be turned.

Turn the cooked crepe out on a oiled plate and continue frying until all the batter is used. Crepes may be filled at once or stored in the refrigerator for later use. They freeze well unfilled, if separated by waxed paper.

Blintzes
12 blintzes

1 recipe cooked pancakes or crepes, about 9 inches in diameter
1 recipe cheese filling (see page 103)

Butter or margarine for frying
Sour cream and preserves, for serving

Fill the pancakes with *uncooked side down.* Fold the sides over the filling and roll the blintzes, making sure that the filling is completely covered. Fry gently in butter until browned on all sides. Serve hot with sour cream and preserves for dessert or a full meal.

OTHER FILLED PANCAKES

Crepes should be served warm or at room temperature. It is best to fill them and then reheat, if reheating is necessary.

Dinner Crepes
Serves 6

1 recipe cooked crepes (see page 104)
1 recipe fish or seafood filling (see page 103) or other pancake filling (see page 102)

2 cups any sauce from Chapter 3
½ cup grated Cheddar or Swiss cheese
2 tablespoons butter or margarine for top

Preheat oven to 350°F. Fill the prepared crepes with 2 or 3 tablespoons of filling. Roll and arrange in a casserole. Top with sauce, sprinkle with cheese and dot with butter. Bake for about 15 minutes, or until browned. Serve at once.

Dessert Crepes   Serves 4 or 6

12 6-inch cooked crepes,   1 to 1½ cups fresh or
   warm or at room   frozen fruit
   temperature
 1 recipe sweet cheese
   filling (see page 104)

Fill the crepes while still hot and arrange on a serving platter or on individual plates. Top with the fruit.

FILLED PASTRY

Use any pastry dough recipe from pages 157–159. From this beginning you can make pasties, knishes, piroshki and probably something of your own design.

Pasties

Pasties are large turnovers filled with potatoes, and other hearty foods. They are wonderful for lunch and dinner, and great for picnics. It is said they originated in the mining towns of Cornwall, England. Miners' wives wrapped them in their aprons and took them to the mines so their men would have a hot meal at noontime.

My mother was raised in Northern Michigan, where mines were aplenty. She grew up on "pasties" and so did I.

4 pasties

 1 recipe pastry for a   1 recipe pastry filling #1 or
   double-crust pie (see   #2 (see pages 102, 103)
   page 157)   Butter for top

Preheat oven to 350°F. Divide the dough into 4 parts. Roll into a circle about ⅛ inch thick. Spread about ⅔ to 1 cup of filling on one half of each round. Dot with butter. Fold the other pastry half over and seal the edges by pinching between thumb and forefinger. Place on baking sheets and bake until the pastry is cooked, about 20 to 25 minutes. Serve hot or cold.

Knishes

About 10

1 recipe pastry for a
double-crust pie (see
page 157)
1 recipe pastry filling #1
or #2 (see pages 102, 103)

¼ to ½ cup melted butter
or margarine

Preheat oven to 350°F. Roll out the dough into a rectangle about ⅛ inch thick and cut into 5-inch squares. Place ¼ cup filling in the center of each square. Fold the sides over the filling and roll up.

Brush liberally with melted butter. Bake on a cookie sheet for about 30 minutes, or until browned. Serve as a main course with vegetable and salad.

Piroshki

Piroshki may only be a knish by another name, but the shape is different. Follow the rules for knish, but form the dough into circles. Fill one half, fold the other pastry half over it, forming a half-moon shape. Seal the edges with a fork. Bake on a cookie sheet in a 350°F. oven for about 30 minutes, or until browned.

Serve with soups instead of bread, or make them very tiny and serve as an appetizer.

MAIN DISHES

Try any of these recipes for a change of pace in your daily meal planning.

STUFFED CABBAGE ROLLS

12 to 14 rolls

1 medium-sized cabbage
2 tablespoons oil
1 large onion, chopped
¼ cup uncooked rice
2 cups firm tofu, crumbled, or 1 cup firm plus 1 cup rehydrated PSP (see page 9)
2 eggs
2 teaspoons salt
1 teaspoon ground cumin
Pepper to taste
2 cups tomato puree
2 cups water
2 bay leaves
4 or 5 whole allspice
1 tablespoon paprika
½ lemon, unpeeled

Cut out the stem out of the cabbage with a sharp, thin-bladed knife. Place cabbage, stem side down, in a large pot with about 2 cups water. Cover tightly and bring to a boil. Cook for about 3 to 5 minutes, just enough to soften the leaves. Remove from heat and set aside.

Heat the oil in the pot you will use for the cabbage rolls and sauté the onion until soft. Put them in a bowl and mix with the rice, tofu, eggs, 1 teaspoon of the salt, cumin, and pepper.

Cool the cabbage leaves in cold water, if they are too hot to handle, and separate them. Place about ¼ cup of the tofu mixture in each leaf. Fold the sides of the cabbage leaf over the stuffing, and roll, beginning at the stem end. Secure with wooden toothpicks. Place the rolls in the pot in which the onions were cooked.

Pour the puree and water over the rolls. Add the bay leaves, allspice, paprika, lemon, the remaining teaspoon salt, and pepper. Cover and bring to a simmer. Reduce the heat and simmer slowly for about 2 hours. The rolls can also be baked in a 300°F. oven for 2 hours.

TOFU STROGANOFF

Serves 6

- 3 tablespoons margarine or oil
- 6 slices firm tofu, about ½ inch thick
- ½ teaspoon salt
- ½ teaspoon poultry seasoning
- ¼ teaspoon pepper
- ¼ teaspoon dried rosemary
- 1 bay leaf
- 1 chicken bouillon cube
- ½ cup hot water

- ½ pound fresh mushrooms, sliced
- 2 tablespoons cornstarch
- ½ cup dry sherry
- 1 cup sour cream
- ½ cup water to thin, if needed
- 3 cups cooked white or brown rice
- Parsley sprigs
- Paprika

Heat the shortening in a large skillet. Arrange the tofu in the pan and fry over a medium heat until nicely browned on one side. Combine the salt, poultry seasoning, pepper, rosemary, and bay leaf in a mortar and grind together until very fine. Turn the tofu slices and sprinkle the ground flavorings over them. Continue frying until both sides are browned. Combine the bouillon cube and water. Spread the mushrooms over the tofu slices and add ¼ cup of the bouillon. Cover and reduce heat to low. Steam for about 5 minutes while you prepare the sauce.

Combine the cornstarch and sherry. Add the remaining ¼ cup bouillon and sour cream. Cook in a saucepan over medium heat until it thickens (*do not boil*). Thin with water, if necessary.

Spread the cooked rice on a heated platter and arrange the tofu slices and mushrooms on top. Pour the sauce over. Sprinkle with paprika and garnish with sprigs of fresh parsley.

MUSHROOM-ARTICHOKE CASSEROLE

Serves 6

2 cups cooked vegetables of any kind, chopped
1 cup cooked rice
½ teaspoon garlic powder
1½ teaspoons salt
½ teaspoon pepper
1 6-ounce jar marinated artichoke hearts
12 ounces firm tofu (4 slices), diced
1 cup diced chicken or turkey meat, (optional)
1 cup grated Swiss cheese
2 tablespoons butter or margarine

½ pound fresh mushrooms, sliced
2 tablespoons cornstarch
¼ cup dry sherry or vermouth
2 tablespoons lemon juice
1 teaspoon dried tarragon
2 teaspoons prepared mustard
1 cup soy milk or dairy milk
2 tablespoons butter for dotting

Preheat oven to 350°F. Combine the vegetables with the rice, garlic, ½ teaspoon salt, and ¼ teaspoon pepper. Spoon into a greased 2-quart casserole and spread evenly over the bottom.

Drain the artichoke hearts and reserve the marinade. Cut hearts into quarters and arrange over the vegetables. Spread the tofu, chicken and half the cheese over the vegetables and artichokes. Set aside.

Melt the butter and sauté the mushrooms for 2 minutes. Dissolve the cornstarch in the sherry and lemon juice. Add the tarragon, mustard, the remaining 1 teaspoon salt and ¼ teaspoon pepper, and milk. Stir into the mushrooms, adding some of the artichoke marinade, or water, to thin to the consistency of heavy cream.

Pour the mushroom mixture over the casserole. Sprinkle with the remaining cheese and dot with butter. Bake for about 30 minutes, or until bubbly and browned. Serve at once.

LEEK AND SWISS CHARD FRITTATA

A frittata is a kind of Italian omelet. Making the frittata with tofu cuts egg use without sacrificing flavor or texture.

Serves 4 to 6

3 medium-sized leeks
3 medium-sized leaves Swiss chard
1 cup soft tofu
1 egg
2 tablespoons cornstarch
¾ cup soy milk or dairy milk
½ teaspoon salt
Pepper to taste
1 teaspoon Worcestershire sauce
¼ cup grated Parmesan cheese

Preheat oven to 350°F. Grease an 8- by 8-inch pan or a 9-inch pie pan. Wash and clean leeks and chard and cut into small pieces. Steam or boil until fully cooked.

Combine the tofu, egg, cornstarch, milk, salt, pepper, and Worcestershire sauce in a blender jar and blend until smooth.

Spread the cooked vegetables over the bottom of the prepared pan. Pour the tofu mixture over the vegetables. Sprinkle with cheese. Bake for 20 to 30 minutes, or until the top is brown and crusty.

BROCCOLI-FILLED MUSHROOMS

Serves 6

¼ cup bread crumbs
1 pound large mushrooms
1 10-ounce package frozen chopped broccoli
1 cup soft tofu
1 tablespoon chopped onion
1 large clove garlic, chopped fine
1 tablespoon lemon juice
1 teaspoon dried basil
½ teaspoon salt, or to taste
½ teaspoon pepper
2 tablespoons oil

Preheat oven to 350°F. Grease a casserole and sprinkle with the bread crumbs. Wash the mushrooms, remove stems, and chop. Arrange the caps, top side down, in the prepared casserole (the mushrooms should be very close together).

Thaw and drain the broccoli. Mash the tofu with a fork and combine with the broccoli, onion, garlic, lemon juice, basil, salt, and pepper. Taste and correct seasoning.

Fill the mushroom caps with the broccoli mixture and fill the spaces between with any filling that is left over. Dribble the oil over the top.

Bake until the mushrooms are soft, about 30 minutes. Serve as the main course with potatoes or rice and a salad.

ZUCCHINI OMELET

Serves 4

3 small zucchini (about ½ pound)	2 eggs
	3 slices bread
1½ teaspoons salt	½ cup soy milk or dairy
1 onion, chopped	milk
2 tablespoons butter or margarine	½ cup grated Parmesan cheese
1 cup soft tofu	¼ teaspoon pepper

Grate the zucchini and place in a bowl. Sprinkle with 1 teaspoon salt and set aside for 15 minutes. Drain, rinse, and dry thoroughly.

In a skillet sauté the onion in butter until translucent. Add the zucchini and cook for 3 minutes.

Mash the tofu in a bowl. Add the eggs and beat together. Cut the bread into cubes and soak them in the milk. Spoon into the tofu mixture and stir in the cheese, the remaining ½ teaspoon salt, and pepper. Add to the zucchini and onion and cook gently over low heat, pulling toward the center with a fork. Cook the omelet until it is well set. Place under the broiler to brown.

Serve as a main course with sliced tomatoes and potatoes or rice.

EGGPLANT CREPES

Serves 6

1 eggplant (about 1 pound)
1 tablespoon oil
1 10-ounce package
   frozen spinach, cooked
   and drained
1 large clove garlic,
   chopped fine
2 tablespoons chopped
   parsley
1 cup firm tofu, mashed
1 cup yogurt, cottage
   cheese, or ricotta

½ teaspoon dried oregano
½ teaspoon salt
   Pepper to taste
1 to 2 cups tomato sauce
   (see page 119)
½ cup grated cheese of
   your choice
   Butter to dot top of
   casserole

Preheat oven to 350°F. Cut the top and bottom from the eggplant. Slice it lengthwise as thinly as possible. Coat slices with oil on one side and arrange on a cookie sheet. Bake until the slices are soft enough to roll, about 10 minutes.

Combine the spinach, garlic, parsley, tofu, yogurt, oregano, salt, and pepper in a bowl and mix well.

When the eggplant slices are soft, fill each with a tablespoon or two of the spinach mixture. Roll and place in a baking dish side by side.

Top with tomato sauce, grated cheese and dots of butter. Bake for about 30 minutes, or until bubbly and brown.

POTATOES AND TOFU GRATIN DAUPHINOISE

Serves 6

6 to 8 new potatoes
3 tablespoons butter
1 clove garlic, slivered
⅛ teaspoon nutmeg
1 egg
½ cup soy milk or dairy milk
4 to 6 (½-inch) slices soft tofu

Salt and pepper to taste
1 cup grated Cheddar or Swiss cheese
1 tablespoon butter for topping

Preheat oven to 350°F. Slice the potatoes, peeled or unpeeled, and soak in cold water. Melt the butter in a casserole and sauté the garlic for a minute or two. Discard the garlic.

Combine the nutmeg, egg, and milk and beat well. Drain the potatoes. Make a layer of half of the potatoes in the casserole. Top with sliced tofu. Add salt and pepper to taste. Top tofu with the remaining potatoes and pour over the egg-milk mixture. Sprinkle with cheese. Salt and pepper again and dot with butter.

Bake for about 1 hour, or until potatoes are cooked and casserole is brown and crusty. Serve immediately with a green salad and whole-grain bread.

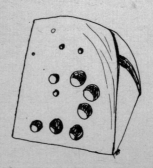

TOFU FLORENTINE

Serves 6

3 10-ounce packages
frozen chopped spinach
6 tablespoons margarine or
butter
1 large clove garlic,
chopped very fine
1 medium-sized onion,
chopped
¼ teaspoon salt
Pepper to taste
1 pound fresh mushrooms,
sliced
3 tablespoons flour

1 2-ounce to 4-ounce can
chopped black olives
1½ cups chicken or beef
stock
¼ cup soy milk or dairy
milk
3 tablespoons lemon juice
Dash of cinnamon
2 to 3 cups cubed firm
tofu, marinated if
desired (see page 40)
1 cup grated Cheddar or
Swiss cheese

Thaw and drain the spinach. Melt 3 tablespoons of the margarine and sauté the garlic and onion until onion is limp. Mix in the drained spinach and season with salt and pepper. Cook, stirring, until all water is evaporated. Arrange spinach around the edge of a large, shallow casserole or baking dish.

Melt the remaining 3 tablespoons of margarine and sauté the mushrooms for 3 minutes. Sprinkle in the flour and cook, stirring, for another minute or two. Add the olives. Gradually add the stock and milk, and cook until the mixture thickens. Add the lemon juice and cinnamon. Taste and correct seasoning. Mix in the tofu cubes and ½ cup of the cheese. Spoon the mushrooms into the center of the baking dish. Sprinkle over the rest of the cheese. Place dish under the broiler and cook until it is nicely browned. Serve at once.

POTATO CASSEROLE

Serves 6

6 medium-sized potatoes
6 slices bacon
1 medium-sized onion, sliced very thin
6 (¼-inch) slices firm tofu
1 cup shredded Cheddar cheese

Salt and pepper to taste
1 cup soy milk or dairy milk
3 tablespoons butter or margarine
Sour cream

Preheat oven to 350°F. Wash and slice the potatoes about ⅛-inch thick (the potatoes need not be peeled). Cover with cold water and set aside.

Cut the bacon into ½-inch squares and fry until very crisp. Drain on paper towels.

Grease a shallow 2-quart casserole. Arrange half the potato slices on the bottom. Top with the onion slices and then the tofu slices. Sprinkle with ¾ cup of the cheese, half the bacon squares and salt and pepper to taste. Arrange the remaining potatoes on top, sprinkle on the remaining cheese and bacon squares. Add more salt and pepper, and pour the milk into the casserole, being careful not to disturb the toppings. Dot with the butter.

Bake for 45 to 55 minutes, or until the potatoes are cooked. Serve with sour cream for a topping.

STUFFED BAKED APPLES

Serves 6

6 large baking apples
¾ cup sugar
⅓ cup raisins
½ cup cooked rice
½ cup soft tofu, mashed

¼ cup melted butter
¼ teaspoon salt
Cinnamon to taste
2 cups water

Preheat oven to 350°F. Butter a baking dish. Wash the apples well and cut a large slice from the top of each. Reserve the top. Scoop out the center of the apples, leaving a large well (be careful not to break the skin). A spoon works very well for this. Sprinkle each with 1 teaspoon of the sugar.

Combine ¼ cup of the sugar with the raisins, rice, tofu, butter, and salt, mixing well. Stuff the apples and sprinkle with cinnamon. Cap with the reserved tops.

Place close together in the prepared dish. Sprinkle with the remaining sugar. Add the water and bake for 45 minutes, or until the apples are soft. Baste often.

Serve with roast meats or as a garnish to a vegetarian curry. Also serve as a dessert with a vanilla or lemon sauce.

CAULIFLOWER MOUSSE

Serves 6 to 8

2 pounds cauliflower	1 cup soft tofu
½ pounds white mushrooms	1 egg, (optional)
½ cup finely chopped onion	¼ cup soy milk or dairy milk
2 tablespoons butter or margarine	1 teaspoon cornstarch
½ teaspoon salt	1 teaspoon Worcestershire sauce
Pepper to taste	¼ cup bread crumbs

Preheat oven to 350°F. Wash the cauliflower and break apart. Boil or steam until soft. Drain. Reserve 6 florets and finely chop the rest.

Chop the mushrooms and squeeze out the water by twisting them in a towel. Sauté with the onion in butter until cooked and quite dry. Stir in the salt and pepper.

Combine the tofu, egg, milk, cornstarch, and Worcestershire sauce in the blender and blend until smooth. Now combine the tofu mixture, cauliflower, mushrooms, and bread crumbs together. Taste and correct for seasoning. Pour into an oiled casserole or tube mold. Place the casserole in a larger pan. Add about an inch of boiling water to the larger pan. Bake for about 25 minutes, or until firm. Unmold and decorate with the reserved florets. Serve hot as a vegetable or cold as a salad.

MALFATTI (Spinach Dumplings)

18 to 20 dumplings

½ cup cooked chopped spinach
¾ cup firm tofu, crumbled
3 tablespoons flour
¼ cup bread crumbs
1 egg
¼ cup Parmesan cheese
½ cup minced onion
1 clove garlic, chopped

½ teaspoon salt
Dash of nutmeg
Pepper to taste
2 cups tomato sauce (see page 119)
Grated Swiss, Cheddar, or Parmesan cheese for topping

Combine the spinach, tofu, flour, bread crumbs, egg, cheese, onion, garlic, salt, nutmeg, and pepper in the food processor or a mixing bowl and beat until well mixed.

Form a tablespoonful into a 3-inch roll. (Flour your hands for easier handling.) Wrap and chill for several hours or freeze for future use.

To cook, heat about 2 inches of water in a large skillet. Reduce to a simmer and add the malfatti carefully. Poach for 3 or 4 minutes. When they are cooked they will rise to the top of water. Remove with a slotted spoon to a heated platter or a shallow casserole.

Pour tomato sauce over the malfatti and sprinkle with grated cheese. (The prepared casserole can be frozen for future use.) Place under the broiler until the cheese is bubbly and serve immediately.

ITALIAN-STYLE TOMATO SAUCE

2 quarts

3 large onions, chopped
1 stalk celery, chopped
1 green pepper, seeded and chopped
2 large cloves garlic, chopped fine
4 tablespoons olive oil
1 teaspoon salt
1 teaspoon pepper
6 whole allspice

1 bay leaf
½ teaspoon dried oregano
½ teaspoon dried basil
1 28-ounce can tomato puree or sauce
1 6-ounce can tomato paste
1 cup dry red or rosé wine, or 1 cup water and 1 tablespoon vinegar

Using a large, heavy-bottomed pot or skillet, sauté the onion, celery, pepper, and garlic in the oil, cooking until the onion is translucent and limp. Add the seasonings: salt, pepper, allspice, bay leaf, oregano, and basil and stir well. Cook for 1–2 minutes.

Add the tomato puree and paste, and the wine. Bring to a slow simmer and cook for at least 2 hours. Serve on any pasta dish or use in casseroles.

MEAT AND TOFU LOAF

Serves 6 to 8

1 pound ground beef
1 pound firm tofu, or 2 cups frozen, thawed, squeezed tofu
½ cup okara, or ⅓ cup bread crumbs
2 eggs
¼ teaspoon ground cloves
⅛ teaspoon ground nutmeg
½ teaspoon salt

¼ teaspoon pepper
2 tablespoons oil
½ cup chopped celery
1 medium-sized onion, chopped
1 carrot, chopped
¼ cup chopped parsley
2 bouillon cubes, dissolved in ¼ cup hot water

Preheat oven to 350°F. Combine the beef, tofu, okara, eggs, cloves, nutmeg, salt, and pepper in a bowl and beat well.

Heat the oil in a skillet and sauté the celery, onion, and carrot until partly cooked. Add the parsley and the bouillon, mix well, then add the vegetables to the meat/tofu mixture. Mix well. Form into a loaf and bake in a 5- by 9-inch loaf pan, or a square baking pan, about 1 hour until very brown. Serve with a sauce of your choice.

This loaf is excellent cold for sandwiches.

PSP BALLS

¾ cup PSP tofu (see page 9)
¾ cup hot water
2 tablespoons olive oil
1 large clove garlic, chopped
½ cup bread crumbs

2 tablespoons flour
¼ cup grated Parmesan cheese
½ teaspoon salt
½ teaspoon pepper
1 egg
¼ cup parsley flakes

Combine the tofu with the water, oil, and garlic and set aside for several minutes. Add the bread crumbs, flour, cheese, salt, and pepper, mixing well. Then stir in the egg and parsley. Refrigerate the mixture for at least 1 hour before using. The mixture should be the consistency of meat balls. If it is too sticky, add more bread crumbs. If it is too dry, add water.

Form into balls of whatever size you like. They may be fried until golden brown or baked in a 350°F. oven until they are brown and crusty, about 45 minutes for 2-inch PSP balls.

Serve with Italian tomato sauce (see page 119).

8

TOFU FOR BREAKFAST AND BRUNCH

TOFU FOR BREAKFAST

In the really great breakfast preparations, tofu can be used instead of eggs. The results are at once delicious and surprising. I had always thought it necessary to use beaten egg whites to make things light. I was wrong.

Waffles made with tofu are crisp and light; pancakes are light and have excellent texture. Try these eggless recipes when you are entertaining and tell your guests about tofu—or don't tell them and smile to yourself as you accept their compliments.

Using tofu with eggs in some of the traditional egg preparations allows you to cut out half of the eggs, and half the cholesterol content as well.

SCRAMBLED TOFU

Serves 4

1 cup firm tofu	Salt
4 eggs	1 tablespoon oil or butter

Mash the tofu with a fork or potato masher. Beat the eggs lightly and combine with the tofu. Salt to taste. Heat the oil in a skillet. Pour in the tofu-egg mixture and cook, stirring constantly. Serve as you would scrambled eggs, with all the trimmings.

Variations:

1. Scrambled tofu with bacon: Fry 4 slices of bacon very crisp. Break into bits and add to scrambled tofu-eggs after they are cooked.
2. Scrambled tofu with lox:* Cut ⅛ pound of lox into small pieces. Mix with tofu-eggs before cooking. Cook as directed.
3. Scrambled tofu with onion: Chop 1 small onion and sauté in oil until soft. Add the tofu-egg mixture and cook to your taste.
4. Scrambled tofu with sausage: Break or cut sausage into small pieces and fry until done. Add the tofu-egg mixture and cook, stirring, until done.

WAFFLES AND PANCAKES

There are two very different ways to make these breakfast favorites. They can be made with yeast or with baking powder as the leavening agents.

Making waffles and pancakes with yeast takes some forethought. It is best to start them the day before you wish to serve them. Baking powder recipes can be made on the spur of the moment.

When yeast is used, the salt (sodium) content is reduced to almost nothing. Baking powder preparations are very high in salt.

The yeast waffles and pancakes are especially delicious and are well worth the extra attention.

* Lox = salted and smoked salmon

YEAST WAFFLES

6 waffles

¼ cup warm water
1 package (1 tablespoon) active dry yeast
1 teaspoon sugar
4 tablespoons softened shortening
1 cup scalded soy milk or dairy milk

½ cup soft tofu
½ cup water
1½ cups flour
¼ teaspoon salt
Milk to thin, if necessary

Combine the ¼ cup of warm water, yeast, and sugar. If the yeast is live, it will foam in a minute or two.

Add the shortening to the milk, stirring until the shortening melts. Cool. Combine the tofu with ½ cup of water and the yeast mixture in a blender jar and beat until smooth. Add this to the milk and beat with the flour and salt.

Cover and place in a draft-free place to rise (it can be left overnight).

When the batter has doubled in bulk, possibly on the next morning, punch down and leave it to rise again while you get all the other breakfast preparations under way. By the time the waffle iron is hot, and the syrup is on the table, you can begin to bake the waffles.

Yeast Waffle Variations:

1. Whole-wheat waffles: Use 1¼ cups whole-wheat flour instead of all-purpose flour.
2. Cornmeal waffles: Use ¼ cup yellow cornmeal and 1¼ cups all-purpose flour.
3. Nut waffles: Add ½ cup chopped nuts to the basic recipe just before baking the waffles.
4. Sesame waffles: Sprinkle sesame seeds over the batter after you have poured it on the waffle iron grid, then bake as usual. Do *not* mix the seeds into the batter.
5. Mixed flour waffles: Mix different kinds of flour together to total 1⅓ cups. Use wheat, rye, corn, rice, etc.
6. Okara or bran waffles: Add ¼ to ½ cup okara or bran to the basic recipe and a bit more moisture, if needed.
7. Wheat germ waffles: Add ¼ cup wheat germ to the

basic recipe, and more milk or water as needed to thin.

YEAST PANCAKES

24 pancakes

¼ cup warm water	2 tablespoons oil
1 package (1 tablespoon) active dry yeast	½ cup soft tofu
1 teaspoon sugar	½ teaspoon salt
1½ cups soy milk, dairy milk, or water	1½ cups flour

Start the night before you wish to serve the pancakes. Combine the warm water, yeast, and sugar. It will foam if it is live; if it doesn't, the pancakes will not rise.

Combine the milk, oil, tofu, and salt, and mix either with a rotary beater or a food processor. Add the yeast mixture and then the flour, beating well. Cover and place in a draft-free place to rise overnight.

Punch down in the morning and allow to rise again while you prepare the rest of breakfast. Bake 4-inch pancakes on a lightly oiled griddle. Serve them with syrup or jam.

Yeast Pancakes Variations:

1. Raisin-nut pancakes: Add ¼ cup raisins and ¼ cup chopped nuts just before baking the pancakes.
2. Whole-wheat pancakes: Use 1¼ cups whole-wheat flour in place of all-purpose flour.
3. Bran or okara pancakes: Add ¼ to ½ cup unprocessed bran or okara to the basic recipe and add more moisture, if needed.
4. Wheat germ pancakes: Add ¼ cup wheat germ to the basic recipe and more liquid, if needed.
5. Corn fritters: Add 1 cup of well-drained, whole-kernel corn to the recipe just before baking.

6. Mixed-flour pancakes: Use 1⅓ cups of mixed flour in any proportions instead of white flour. Possibilities are whole-wheat, rye, cornmeal, rice, barley, etc.

PLAIN WAFFLES OR PANCAKES

6 waffles or 24 pancakes

½ cup soft tofu
1½ cups buttermilk
1 tablespoon baking powder
½ teaspoon baking soda
2 tablespoons sugar
½ cup okara or unprocessed bran

½ teaspoon salt
¼ cup oil for pancakes or ⅓ cup oil for waffles or melted butter
1½ cups flour

Combine the tofu, buttermilk, baking powder, soda, sugar, okara, and salt in a blender jar or food processor bowl and beat until smooth. Add the oil.

Pour into a mixing bowl and stir in the flour. Do not beat. Bake on a preheated waffle iron or on a lightly oiled griddle. Serve with jam, syrup, honey, or applesauce.

WHEAT AND BRAN PANCAKES

15 to 20 pancakes

½ cup soft tofu
1½ cups soy milk or dairy milk
¼ cup melted butter or oil
½ teaspoon salt
2 tablespoons sugar

1 tablespoon baking powder
¾ cup unprocessed bran
¾ cup all-purpose flour
½ cup whole-wheat flour
¼ cup wheat germ

Combine tofu, milk, butter, salt, sugar, and baking powder in a blender jar or food processor bowl and blend until smooth. Pour into a mixing bowl and add the bran, flours, and wheat germ, stirring until just moistened.

Bake on a lightly oiled griddle and serve with jam, syrup, or honey.

RICE FLOUR WAFFLES OR PANCAKES

4 waffles or 20 pancakes

For the dieter or the hyperallergic, here is a breakfast treat without eggs, wheat or cholesterol. And they are just delicious, too.

½ cup soft tofu
1½ cups buttermilk or
   soured milk
½ cup okara (optional)
1 tablespoon baking
   powder

½ teaspoon baking soda
2 tablespoons sugar
⅓ cup oil for waffles or ¼
   cup oil for pancakes
½ teaspoon salt
2 cups rice flour

Combine the tofu, buttermilk, okara, baking powder, soda, sugar, oil, and salt in a blender jar or food processor bowl and blend until very smooth. Transfer to a bowl and beat in the rice flour. Batter should be thinner for pancakes than for waffles. If too thick, beat in more buttermilk.

Bake on a lightly oiled griddle or a preheated waffle iron. Serve with syrup, heated honey, or jam. They are especially good with apple butter.

CORNMEAL WAFFLES

4 to 6 waffles

½ cup soft tofu
2 cups buttermilk
1 tablespoon baking powder
½ teaspoon baking soda
1 tablespoon sugar
⅓ cup oil, or melted butter or margarine
½ teaspoon salt
¼ cup okara or unprocessed bran or wheat germ
1 cup flour
¾ cup cornmeal

Combine the tofu, buttermilk, baking powder, soda, sugar, oil, salt, and okara in a blender jar or food processor bowl. Blend until smooth.

Pour into a mixing bowl. Mix in the flour and cornmeal. Bake on a preheated waffle iron. The recipe will make 4 large square waffles or 6 round waffles.

Serve with heated honey or syrup.

TOFU FOR BRUNCH

The following recipes are for more complex preparations that can serve for brunch or for light suppers. They are excellent for breakfast, too, or for an after-theater snack.

POTATO PANCAKES

10 to 14 pancakes

2 cups grated raw potatoes
½ cup soft tofu
1 teaspoon salt
¼ cup flour
1 teaspoon baking powder
1 medium-sized onion, grated (optional)
Oil for frying

The potatoes should be grated and then soaked in water to remove excess starch, otherwise the pancakes are liable to be green.

Combine the tofu, salt, flour, and baking powder in a blender jar and blend until smooth. Pour into a mixing bowl. Drain the potatoes and add to the tofu mixture. Stir in the onion.

Fry the pancakes on a griddle or iron spider in a generous amount of oil over medium heat. Serve with sour cream and applesauce.

POACHED TOFU WITH HAM BÉARNAISE

Serves 6

1 teaspoon salt
6 2½ x 2½-inch squares of soft tofu ½-inch thick
6 thin slices of ham (Smithfield preferred)

3 English muffins, halved, toasted and buttered
1 recipe béarnaise sauce (see page 46)

Cover bottom of a skillet with about 1 inch of water. Add salt and bring to a boil. Carefully place the tofu slices in the water. Poach over medium heat for 5 minutes, or until tofu becomes puffy.

On the individual heated serving plates, place a toasted English muffin half. Top with a slice of ham and a tofu slice. Cover with béarnaise sauce and garnish with a sprig of fresh parsley.

TOFU AND CREAMY ONIONS

Serves 6

1½ pounds yellow onions
4 tablespoons margarine or butter or oil
4 tablespoons flour
2 cups hot soy milk or dairy milk
1 teaspoon salt

¼ teaspoon pepper
Pinch of fresh nutmeg
6 2½ x 2½-inch squares of soft tofu, ½-inch thick
Sweet pickle slices
Toasted bread or English muffins

Slice the onions into rounds about ¼-inch thick. Melt the shortening in a large skillet and cook the onions for about

20 minutes, or until soft. Sprinkle the flour over the onions, mixing well. Cook for a minute or two, then add the milk, ½ teaspoon of the salt, pepper, and nutmeg, stirring until the sauce thickens.

Simmer the tofu slices in water with the remaining ½ teaspoon of salt for about 5 minutes, or until they are puffy. Drain the tofu on paper towels and place on a slice of toast on an individual serving plate or on a large serving platter. Cover with onion sauce and garnish with pickle slices.

HAM AND EGG BURGERS

Serves 4

1 cup diced cooked ham
1 cup tofuburger mix (see page 65)
1 tablespoon chopped parsley
4 eggs

Combine the ham, tofuburger, and parsley and form into 4 patties. Fry in oil or bake in a preheated 350°F. oven about 45 minutes until crisp and brown.

Poach the eggs and place on top of the ham patties. Serve with toasted bread or English muffins.

PORK SAUSAGE PATTIES

10 to 12 patties

½ pound sausage meat
1 recipe tofuburger mix (see page 65)
½ teaspoon dried sage
1 teaspoon dry mustard

Combine all the ingredients and form into patties. *Do not taste before cooking.*

Fry in a small amount of fat until very brown. Serve with breakfast foods, such as pancakes or waffles, or serve as a burger on a bun.

9

BAKING WITH TOFU

There are two kinds of bread and they can be made to perfection with tofu instead of eggs: quick breads and yeast breads. Quick breads rely on baking powder and baking soda to make them rise. Yeast breads use yeast.

Quick breads are just that, quick. You decide now that you want bread for supper and in an hour it is done.

Yeast breads take time to rise and cannot be made on the spur of the moment. You can, however, leave yeast dough overnight for baking the next day. This cannot be done with baking powder preparations.

Some quick breads answer to the name cake, such as Carrot Cake or Poppy Seed Cake. They could be called bread just as well.

Tofu does not work well in very light cakes, such as Lady Baltimore or the traditional layer cake. It does its best work in those cakes or breads that are moister and heavier.

The rule for substituting tofu for eggs in quick breads is: ¼ cup mashed tofu = 1 whole egg. Add 1 teaspoon baking powder to the basic recipe.

Tofu can be added to yeast breads as well. It can be an egg substitute, if the recipe calls for egg. Otherwise, it will add protein to the bread without changing the results.

In yeast breads much value is gained from adding okara to the recipe. This will provide protein, texture, fiber and will help the bread stay fresh longer.

If you have no okara on hand, because you have not yet become a tofu maker, you can get it from a shop that makes tofu. I am lucky enough to live near two tofu shops so if I don't have time to make tofu I can get it for a very low price from the tofu shop.

In recipes calling for okara, unprocessed bran can be used. Add a bit more moisture to the recipe, if you do use bran.

ORANGE-NUT MUFFINS

12 muffins

1 small orange, uneeled	½ teaspoon salt
½ cup soft tofu	¼ cup sugar
2 tablespoons oil	¼ teaspoon cinnamon
¾ cup buttermilk	2½ teaspoons baking powder
1 teaspoon vanilla	½ teaspoon baking soda
¼ cup okara or	⅓ cup raisins
unprocessed bran	½ cup chopped nuts
1½ cups all-purpose flour	

Preheat oven to 400°F. Cut the orange in wedges, rind and all, and put it in a blender jar with the tofu, oil, buttermilk, vanilla, and okara. Blend only until the orange is cut in pieces about the size of a rice grain (do not overblend).

Combine the flour, salt, sugar, cinnamon, baking powder, soda, raisins, and nuts in a mixing bowl and add the tofu mixture all at once. Stir together quickly. Spoon into greased or paper-lined 2-inch muffin tins and bake for 20 to 25 minutes. Cool on a rack.

CARROT CAKE

10 to 12 servings

1½ cups flour
½ cup okara or
   unprocessed bran
2 teaspoons baking powder
½ teaspoon baking soda
1 teaspoon cinnamon
¼ teaspoon salt
½ cup shortening
½ cup brown sugar

1 cup soft tofu
2 tablespoons warm water
   (approximately)
1 teaspoon vanilla
1½ cups grated carrot
½ cup raisins
½ cup chopped nuts or
   sunflower seeds, or a
   combination

Preheat oven to 350°F. Grease an 8- by 8-inch pan. Combine the flour, okara, baking powder, soda, cinnamon, and salt in a bowl and mix together.

Using a food processor, a blender, or a rotary beater, combine the shortening, sugar, tofu, water, and vanilla, mixing well. Add the dry ingredients, a little at a time, and mix until smooth. If the batter is too thick to beat or blend easily, add more water.

Stir in the carrot, raisins, and nuts. Spoon the batter into the prepared pan and bake for about 45 minutes, or until the center springs back when touched. Cool on a rack. Serve frosted or unfrosted, as desired.

Cream Cheese Frosting

2 cups confectioners' sugar
⅓ cup very soft butter
⅓ cup soft tofu
1 (3-ounce) package cream
   cheese or ⅓ cup

1 tablespoon lemon juice
1 teaspoon vanilla
Pinch of salt

Sift the sugar and set aside. Blend the remaining ingredients, either by hand or in a food processor. Combine with the confectioners' sugar, adding very hot water, by drops, to thin to the proper consistency for spreading. Frost the cake when it is completely cooled.

POPPY SEED CAKE

Serves 8 to 10

1 cup soft tofu
1 cup sugar
½ cup melted margarine or oil
½ teaspoon salt
2 teaspoons baking powder
¼ teaspoon baking soda
1 teaspoon vanilla
½ cup okara or unprocessed bran (optional)

1 cup soy milk or dairy milk
2½ cups flour (if whole-wheat use 2¼ cups)
½ to 1 cup poppy seeds

Preheat oven to 350°F. Grease an 8-inch tube pan or a 5-by 9-inch bread pan. Combine tofu, sugar, margarine, salt, baking powder, soda, vanilla, and okara in a blender jar or food processor bowl and blend thoroughly. If the mixture is too thick, add some of the milk. (You can also use a rotary mixer or beat by hand.)

Transfer the mixture to a bowl and add the flour and remainder of milk alternately, mixing well after each addition.

Add the poppy seeds last, in whatever quantity you like. Some people like more seeds than cake.

Spoon the batter into the prepared pan. Bake for about 55 minutes, or until the center springs back when pressed. Cool for about 5 minutes on a rack, then remove from the pan to finish cooling. Dust with confectioners' sugar while still warm.

NUT AND SEED CAKE

Serves 8 to 10

1 cup soft tofu
½ cup shortening
½ cup soured milk or
  buttermilk
¼ teaspoon salt
½ teaspoon baking soda
1 tablespoon baking
  powder
1½ teaspoons vanilla
½ cup sugar

¼ cup okara or
  unprocessed bran
¼ teaspoon cinnamon
  (optional)
2 cups all-purpose flour
1 cup chopped nuts and/or
  whole seeds
½ cup raisins
  Confectioners' sugar

Preheat oven to 350°F. Grease an 8- or 9-inch tube pan. Combine the tofu and shortening and beat together well, either with a food processor or rotary mixer. Add the milk, salt, soda, baking powder, vanilla, sugar, okara and cinnamon, beating well again.

Mix in the flour quickly (do not overbeat). If the mixture is too thick, add more milk. The batter should be quite stiff; spoonable, not pourable. Stir in the seeds and raisins.

Spoon into the prepared pan and bake for about 50 minutes, or until the center springs back when pressed. Cool on a rack for about 10 minutes, then remove from the pan. Dust with confectioners' sugar while still warm.

FRUIT BREAD

1 loaf

⅓ cup soft tofu
½ cup soy milk or dairy
   milk
¼ cup soft shortening
1 teaspoon vanilla
½ to ⅔ cup sugar, or to taste
2½ teaspoons baking powder
½ teaspoon baking soda
¼ teaspoon salt
½ teaspoon cinnamon
   (optional)

⅓ cup okara or
   unprocessed bran
2 cups all-purpose flour
1 cup fruit pulp or puree
   (applesauce, prune
   pulp, drained canned
   fruit, or chopped fresh
   fruit of any kind)
½ cup nuts or seeds
¼ to ½ cup raisins

Preheat oven to 350°F. Grease a 5- by 9-inch bread pan. Combine the tofu, milk, shortening, vanilla, and sugar in a blender jar and beat well. In a separate bowl combine the baking powder, soda, salt, cinnamon, okara, and flour. Stir in the tofu mixture and the fruit. If the batter is too thick, add more fruit or more milk (do not overbeat). Stir in the nuts and raisins.

Pour into the prepared pan and bake for 50 to 60 minutes, or until the cake springs back when pressed. Cool on a rack for about 5 minutes, then turn out to cool completely.

GRAPE-NUTS® BREAD

Serves 8 to 10

¼ cup melted butter or
   margarine
1 cup buttermilk
½ cup soft tofu
½ cup sugar
1 cup Grape-Nuts® cereal

2 cups flour
1½ teaspoons baking powder
½ teaspoon baking soda
½ teaspoon salt
½ cup raisins, currants, or
   nuts (optional)

Preheat oven to 350°F. Grease an 8- by 8-inch or a 5- by 9-inch bread pan. Combine the butter, buttermilk, and tofu and beat in the sugar. Stir in the cereal and set aside for a few minutes. Combine the flour, baking powder, soda, and salt and quickly mix with the moist cereal mixture (do not overbeat). Stir in the raisins.

Spoon batter into the prepared pan and bake for 45 to 50 minutes, or until brown and crusty. Serve warm or cool with honey or preserves.

READY-BAKE BRAN MUFFINS

Store the batter for these muffins in the refrigerator for up to two weeks and use it whenever you want fresh muffins.

about 2 quarts batter

3 cups unprocessed bran *or* 1½ cups okara and 1½ cups unprocessed bran *or* 1½ cups unprocessed bran and 1½ cups bran cereal *or* any combination of the above to total 3 cups	¾ cup soft tofu
	1 tablespoon baking powder
	1 teaspoon baking soda
	½ to 1 teaspoon salt
	1 cup sugar
	2½ cups flour
1 cup boiling water	1 cup any fruit, drained and diced
2 cups buttermilk	
½ cup oil	

Measure bran (and okara) into a mixing bowl and add boiling water. Stir together and set aside while mixing other ingredients.

Combine buttermilk, oil, tofu, baking powder, soda, salt, and sugar in a blender jar or food processor bowl and blend smooth. You can also use a rotary beater.

Add the buttermilk mixture to the soaked bran and mix together. Add the flour and stir in quickly, until flour is all moistened. Fold in the fruit.

Other fruits, raisins, nuts and seeds can be added to the basic mixture as follows:

To 2½ cups of basic mix add:
  ½ cup raisins or
  ½ cup chopped nuts or
  ½ cup chopped dates or
  ½ cup sunflower seeds, millet, sesame seeds, or
  ¾ cup chopped fresh apple or
  ½ cup fruit puree or
any combination of things you like, up to a total of 1 extra cup.

Grease muffin tins or line with paper cups. Fill each about three-quarters full. Bake at 400°F. for 20 to 25 minutes, or until nicely browned. 2½ cups of batter plus 1 cup of extra fruit, nuts, or seeds will make 12 (2½-inch) muffins.

PUMPKIN BREAD

1 loaf

⅓ cup soft tofu
½ cup buttermilk
¼ cup soft shortening
1 teaspoon vanilla
½ cup sugar
¼ teaspoon salt
1 teaspoon pumpkin pie spice
1 cup cooked pumpkin pulp

2½ teaspoons baking powder
½ teaspoon baking soda
⅓ cup okara or unprocessed bran
2 cups flour
¼ cup raisins
½ cup mixed seeds and/or nuts

Preheat oven to 350°F. Grease a 5- by 9-inch bread pan. Combine the tofu, buttermilk, shortening, and vanilla in a blender bowl and blend until smooth. Pour this mixture into a bowl and add the sugar, salt, spice, pumpkin, mixing well. Then add the baking powder, soda, and okara and mix again. Add the flour all at once and stir in quickly. If the batter is too thick to mix easily, add a bit more buttermilk. Stir in the raisins and nuts.
Spoon into the prepared pan and bake for 55 minutes,

or until the bread springs back when pressed and begins to shrink away from the sides of the pan. Remove to a rack and cool in the pan for about 10 minutes, then turn out to cool completely.

QUICK YEAST BREAD

This bread uses twice the usual amount of yeast and therefore needs to rise only once. It will have a coarser texture than twice-risen bread.

2 loaves or 18 to 38 rolls

1 cup warm water
1 teaspoon sugar
2 packages (2 to 3 tablespoons) active dry yeast
¾ cup soft tofu
1 cup warm soy milk or dairy milk
½ cup okara or unprocessed bran

½ cup softened butter or margarine
1 teaspoon salt
5 to 6 cups all-purpose flour, or a mixture of wheat, whole wheat or rye flours in any proportion

Combine the water, sugar, and yeast. If it foams in a short time, the yeast is live and usable.

Combine the tofu, milk, okara, butter, and salt in a bowl and beat together. Stir in the yeast mixture. Add 2 to 3 cups of flour and beat until the dough is very elastic.

Turn out on a floured board and knead in as much of the remaining flour as you can, kneading for about 10 minutes until the dough is shiny and smooth. (While kneading on the board you can add herbs and flavors such as dry onion and garlic, to taste.)

Form the dough into two loaves or into rolls of any kind or shape you desire. Or, divide the dough and use some for rolls and some for a loaf, or refrigerate half to use the next day for a coffee cake or for sweet rolls.

After forming, cover with a damp cloth and let rise for about 45 minutes to 1 hour until double in size. During the rising time, preheat the oven to 375°F. Bake loaves for about 45 minutes; rolls for about 20 minutes. Tap them; they should sound hollow and be nicely browned. Cool on a rack for about 10 minutes, and then turn out to cool completely.

To make a sweet loaf:
Preheat the oven to 350°F. Roll out half the dough to a ½-inch thickness. Brush with melted butter and sprinkle with:

sugar, brown sugar, or honey, to taste *and*
cinnamon or nutmeg *and*
chopped nuts and raisins *or*
jam or jelly and all or none of the above

Roll the dough lengthwise, pinching the seam. Place in a greased 5- by 9-inch loaf pan. Cover with a cloth and allow to rise in a warm, draft-free place until about doubled in bulk. Bake for 50 minutes, or until nicely browned.

Cool on a rack for about 5 minutes. Turn out and glaze while still hot with ½ cup confectioners' sugar mixed with 1 tablespoon water.

BATTER BREAD

This is a basic recipe for a yeast-leavened bread that can be made quickly and easily and may be flavored in a number of ways. Most batter breads rely on eggs. This recipe uses tofu to do whatever the eggs do.

2 loaves

2 packages (2 tablespoons) active dry yeast
½ cup warm water
1 teaspoon sugar
1½ cups soy milk or dairy milk
½ cup soft tofu

½ cup okara (optional)
2 tablespoons oil or melted butter
1 teaspoon salt
Choice of flavors given below, or none at all
3½ to 4 cups flour

Combine the yeast and water and prove with the sugar. If it foams in a minute or two, it is fresh and live. If not, get some fresh yeast.

Heat milk to scalding. Cool slightly and place in blender jar with tofu, okara, oil, and salt. Blend until smooth.

Transfer to a bowl. When it has cooled to lukewarm, add the yeast mixture and any flavorings you are using. Stir together well. Add about 2 cups of the flour and beat well. Add another 1 to 1½ cups, not more than can be beaten with ease. Beat in as much of the flour as you can, and beat until the batter climbs the beater blades and becomes very elastic. (Batter bread requires no kneading, but must be very well beaten.)

Cover the bowl with a damp towel and allow to rise in a warm, draft-free place for about 1 hour. This batter will rise quickly because of the large amount of yeast, so be careful not to let it overrise. When doubled in bulk, punch down and spoon into greased bread pan or muffin tins. Allow to rise again until double in bulk.

During the second rising preheat the oven to 350°F. Bake for about 45 minutes for loaves, about 20 minutes for rolls, or until they sound hollow when tapped and are nicely browned. Cool for about 10 minutes in the pans and then turn out to cool completely.

For flavor variations, add to the batter:

1 tablespoon caraway seeds, with ½ teaspoon garlic powder and ½ cup grated Cheddar cheese *or*
1 cup grated Parmesan cheese and 3 tablespoons dried minced onion *or*
1 tablespoon dill weed and 2 tablespoons dried onion *or*
½ to 1 cup mixed seeds: celery, anise, poppy, sesame, sunflower, or dill with 2 tablespoons dried onion *or*
½ cup raisins, 1 tablespoon caraway seeds and ¼ cup sugar.

ORANGE SAVARIN

Serves 6 to 8

A savarin is a very rich, very light yeast bread that is traditionally baked in a tube pan, soaked in syrup and served with the center filled with pastry cream. This recipe is remarkable in that it uses no eggs and very little fat.

1 package (1 tablespoon) active dry yeast	4 tablespoons soft margarine
¼ cup warm water	¼ teaspoon salt
⅓ cup plus 1 teaspoon sugar	1 2-inch square of orange rind
½ cup soft tofu	1½ cups flour
2 tablespoons soy milk or dairy milk	¼ cup dried currants or raisins

Dissolve the yeast in the warm water. Add the 1 teaspoon sugar. If it does not foam up within a minute or so, the yeast is dead and will not leaven the bread. If it is good and lively, set the mixture aside.

Combine the tofu, the ⅓ cup sugar, milk, margarine, salt, and orange rind in a blender jar or food processor bowl and blend until the peel is ground. Transfer to a mixing bowl or, if you have a food processor, use it for the beating.

Add the flour all at once and stir until it is all moistened. If beating by hand, beat until your arm breaks and then use the other arm. If using an electric beater, beat until the dough climbs the beaters and becomes very elastic and shiny. In the food processor this work will take about 30 seconds.

Cover the bowl with a clean towel and let dough rise in a warm place for about 2 hours, or until it doubles in bulk. Punch down and knead in the currants. The dough should be very elastic and quite sticky. Do not add extra flour.

Grease a 7-inch round pan or mold with high sides. (A soufflé dish does very well. You may also use an 8-inch tube pan.) Place the dough in the prepared mold. Allow to rise again until doubled in bulk, at least 1 hour. Preheat the oven to 400°F. during the second rising.

Bake for about 20 minutes, or until the bread pulls away from the sides of the pan and the top springs back when pressed. Cool on a wire rack for about 5 minutes and turn out to cool. Make a glaze of ¼ cup confectioners' sugar mixed with 1 teaspoon very hot water and pour the glaze over the savarin while it is still hot.

You can also make a rum syrup (see page 143) and soak the cake before serving, in which case it is called a rum baba. Serve with ice cream.

SAVARIN (Sweet batter bread)

Serves 6 to 8

1 package (1 tablespoon) active dry yeast	1 teaspoon vanilla
¼ cup warm water	¼ teaspoon salt
½ cup plus 1 teaspoon sugar	Dash of cinnamon or nutmeg (optional)
½ cup soft tofu	1½ cups flour
4 tablespoons soft margarine	Raisins and nuts (optional)
3 tablespoons soy milk or dairy milk	

Combine the yeast with the warm water. Use the teaspoon of sugar to test the yeast; if it foams quickly it is alive.

Combine the tofu, the ½ cup sugar, margarine, milk, vanilla, salt, and spices in a blender jar and blend until very smooth. Pour into a mixing bowl and add the flour all at once, stirring to moisten it. Beat by hand or with an electric beater for *at least* 5 minutes. (The longer the batter is beaten, the better it will be.)

Cover and let rise in a warm, draft-free place until doubled in bulk, about 2 hours. Punch down and add raisins or nuts. Transfer to a greased baking mold about 6 or 7 inches in diameter. A saucepan will do very well. Cover and let rise again until doubled in bulk. Preheat oven to 350°F. during this time.

Bake for 20 to 25 minutes, or until the bread pulls away from the sides of the pan and the center springs back when pressed. Cool in the mold on a wire rack for about 5 minutes before turning it out on to the rack. Sprinkle with confectioners' sugar while still warm, or use a rum syrup in the traditional way.

Rum Syrup

1 cup sugar	½ cup rum
1 cup water	Fresh or thawed frozen
1 teaspoon anise seeds	fruit
2 cinnamon sticks	Whipped cream or ice
Pinch of nutmeg	cream

Combine the sugar, water, anise seeds, cinnamon, and nutmeg in a saucepan and bring to a boil. Add the rum while it is boiling, lower the heat and cook for another minute. Strain the syrup and discard the spices.

Place the savarin in a bowl, pour the hot syrup over it, and let stand until it is soaked. Cool and serve with fruit, whipped cream, or ice cream.

STOLLEN (A Swedish Christmas Pastry)

2 large loaves

1 cup raisins
1 cup mixed candied fruits, chopped finely
¼ cup orange juice
2 packages (2 tablespoons) active dry yeast
½ cup warm water
½ cup plus 1 teaspoon sugar
½ cup soy milk or dairy milk

1 cup butter, margarine or oil
⅔ cup soft tofu
½ teaspoon salt
1 teaspoon almond extract
1 teaspoon grated lemon rind
4½ to 5½ cups all-purpose flour
½ cup slivered almonds
Melted butter
Confectioners' sugar

Combine raisins, candied fruits, and orange juice and set aside.

Mix yeast, warm water and the 1 teaspoon sugar together. It should foam up in a few minutes. (If not, the yeast is dead and you had better get some fresh yeast.) Set this mixture aside.

Heat the milk to scalding. Add the butter and stir until it is melted. Remove from the heat and stir in the ½ cup sugar. Combine this mixture with the tofu in a blender or food processor and beat until smooth. Add the salt, almond extract, and lemon rind.

Transfer the tofu mixture to a large bowl. Using a rotary beater mix in the yeast; then add 2 cups of flour and beat for about 3 minutes. Mix in the fruit and orange juice, and the almonds. Add 2 more cups of flour and beat until the mixture climbs the beaters and is very elastic.

Turn out on a floured board and knead, adding as much of the remaining flour as needed to make a smooth and elastic dough. Place the dough in a greased bowl, cover with a damp cloth and let rise until doubled in bulk— about 2 hours.

Punch down the dough and divide in half. Roll each half into an oval, about 7 inches by 9 inches. Brush with melted butter and fold about one-third of the oval of dough over the other (Diagram 1) two-thirds so that the top edge is about 1 inch or a bit more from the bottom edge. It will look rather like an ill-formed turnover; this is the traditional shape for a stollen.

Carefully transfer the dough to a greased baking sheet, cover, and let rise in a warm, draft-free place until almost doubled in bulk. Preheat the oven during this second rising to 375°F.

Bake for about 25 minutes, or until loaves give a hollow sound when tapped and are nicely browned.

Remove to a rack, brush with melted butter and dust with confectioners' sugar while still hot.

When completely cool, the loaves can be wrapped and stored for a week or two before eating. They make excellent Christmas gifts.

10

DESSERTS: PIES, PUDDINGS, AND PASTRIES

I must admit to being a dessert addict and, for me, finding tofu has been several dozen kinds of blessing. Not only does using tofu lower calories and, of course, cholesterol, but the desserts are every bit as delicious as those made with the "high sin" ingredients.

Tofu is used instead of eggs in most of these recipes. Where eggs are used, you will use fewer of them. In addition, tofu is used instead of high-cholesterol, high-calorie, and high-priced cream cheese in New York Cheesecake and cheese pies.

I think you will find making desserts with tofu the most rewarding discovery of all.

NEW YORK CHEESECAKE AND OTHER CHEESECAKES

NEW YORK CHEESECAKE

Serves 12

Prepare a crumb crust as follows:

12 2-inch-square graham crackers	¼ cup melted butter or margarine
1 tablespoon honey	

Preheat oven to 400°F. Crush the graham crackers in a blender, food processor or with a rolling pin. Add the honey in a stream while mixing at a slow speed or stirring by hand. Then add the melted butter and mix well with a pastry fork or your fingertips. Pat the crumb mixture into a greased 9-inch springform pan, covering the bottom and part way up the sides. Bake for 10 minutes. Remove to a rack to cool before filling. Reduce the oven heat to 350°F.

Filling

4 eggs, separated	2 cups soft tofu
4 ounces medium or sharp Cheddar cheese	⅔ cup sugar
	⅓ cup all-purpose flour
½ cup melted butter or margarine	2 tablespoons lemon juice
	½ teaspoon salt
½ cup buttermilk, soured milk or yogurt	2 teaspoons vanilla
	½ cup raisins (optional)

Separate the eggs and set the whites aside. Cut the cheese into small pieces. Combine the egg yolks, cheese, butter, and milk in a blender jar or food processor bowl and process until very smooth. Add the tofu, sugar, flour, lemon juice, salt, and vanilla and blend until smooth again. If there is too much batter for the jar, divide it in two parts and mix together after all of it has been blended. Taste the mixture and add more lemon juice, if needed, or more sugar or vanilla to suit your own taste.

Beat the egg whites until very stiff. If you are using raisins, add them to the tofu mixture. Fold the egg whites into the tofu mixture.

Pour the filling into the baked crust. Bake at 350°F. for about 50 minutes, or until a knife blade comes out clean when inserted in the center. Place on a rack to cool. Immediately run a knife blade around the edge of the cake to loosen it from the sides. This will prevent cracks from widening as the cake cools.

When the cake has cooled completely, refrigerate for several hours or overnight before serving.

PUMPKIN CHEESECAKE

Serves 12 or more

Preheat oven to 400°F. Prepare a crumb crust, a pie crust, or a cookie dough crust (see page 158) in a 10-inch springform pan and bake for 10 minutes, or until lightly browned. Cool on a rack while preparing the filling. Reduce the oven heat to 350°F.

Filling

¼ pound medium sharp Cheddar cheese, cut in pieces	½ cup flour
	½ teaspoon salt
	2 teaspoons vanilla
4 eggs, separated	1 tablespoon lemon juice
2 cups soft tofu	1 cup cooked pumpkin
1 cup melted margarine or butter, or 1 cup salad oil	1 teaspoon pumpkin pie spice
1½ cups buttermilk or yogurt	
1 cup sugar	

This is a large recipe. It will be necessary to blend the batter in two parts and combine them together later. First combine the cheese, egg yolks, 1 cup of the tofu, shortening, and ½ cup of the buttermilk in a blender jar or food processor bowl and beat until the cheese is completely pureed. Pour this mixture into a large mixing bowl.

Then combine the remaining tofu and buttermilk with the sugar, flour, salt, vanilla, lemon juice, pumpkin and spice and whip until very smooth. Pour this into the bowl with the cheese mixture and blend together.

Beat the egg whites until very stiff and fold them into the pumpkin mixture. Pour the batter into the baked crust and bake in a 350°F. oven for about 55 minutes, or until a knife inserted in the center comes out clean.

Remove to a rack. Run a knife blade around the edge of the cake to loosen it from the sides of the pan. This will prevent any cracks from widening as the cake cools. When the cake is at room temperature, refrigerate for several hours or overnight before serving.

WESTERN CHEESE PIE

1 (9-inch) pie

1 cup soft tofu
1 cup creamed cottage cheese
½ cup plain or vanilla yogurt
½ cup sugar
1 egg
2 tablespoons cornstarch

¼ teaspoon salt
1 teaspoon vanilla
1 teaspoon lemon juice
Milk to thin, if necessary
1 prebaked crumb crust (see page 160)

Preheat oven to 350°F. Combine tofu, cottage cheese, yogurt, sugar, egg, cornstarch, salt, vanilla, and lemon juice in a blender or food processor and process until very smooth. If the batter is too thick to blend well, add a small amount of milk.

Pour into the pie shell and bake for about 20 to 30 minutes, or until a knife blade inserted in the center comes out *almost* clean. Cool for 5 minutes.

Topping

1½ cups sour cream
1 tablespoon sugar

½ teaspoon vanilla

Combine the ingredients and pour over the warm cheese pie. Return to the oven and bake for just 5 minutes longer. Cool on a rack until it has reached room temperature and then refrigerate for several hours before serving.

CHEESE PIE WITH FRUIT

A favorite treat is cheese pie topped with glazed strawberries or other fruits.

Filling   Serves 8

- 1 9-inch pie crust
- 1 cup soft tofu
- 1 cup creamed cottage cheese
- 1 tablespoon cornstarch
- 1 egg

- 2 teaspoons lemon juice
- ¼ teaspoon grated lemon rind
- ¼ teaspoon salt
- ¼ cup sugar
- 1 teaspoon vanilla

Prebake a single crust for a 9-inch pie for 7 minutes at 400°F. (see page 157). Lower oven heat to 350°F. Combine the filling ingredients in a blender or food processor bowl and puree until very smooth. Pour into the pie shell and bake for 25 to 30 minutes, or until a knife blade comes out *almost* clean when inserted in the center. Cool to room temperature before adding fruit.

1. Strawberry Topping

- 1 pint fresh strawberries or
- 1 10-ounce package of frozen berries, thawed and drained

- ½ cup fruit juice or water
- ¼ cup grenadine syrup
- 1 tablespoon cornstarch
- 2 tablespoons sugar

Arrange the fruit on the pie. Combine the fruit juice, grenadine, cornstarch, and sugar and heat until the mixture thickens. Cool to lukewarm and pour over the pie, coating the fruit completely. Refrigerate for several hours before serving.

2. Raspberry Topping

- 1 10-ounce package frozen raspberries, well drained
- ¾ cup juice (dilute raspberry juice with water to measure ¾ cup)

- 2 tablespoons grenadine syrup
- 1 tablespoon cornstarch
- 2 tablespoons sugar

Drain raspberries and set aside. Combine the juice with grenadine and add the cornstarch and sugar. Mix well and then heat until it thickens. Cool to lukewarm and stir in the raspberries. Spoon over the cheese pie. Refrigerate for several hours before serving.

3. Blueberry Topping

1 1-pound can blueberries, well drained	1 tablespoon cornstarch
¾ cup blueberry syrup from can	2 tablespoons sugar

Drain blueberries and set aside. Mix the syrup with cornstarch and sugar. Cook until thickened, then mix with the berries. Cool to lukewarm and spoon over the cheese pie. Refrigerate for several hours before serving.

EASY LEMON CHEESECAKE

Serves 8 or more

1 crumb crust	¼ teaspoon salt
1 package lemon-flavored gelatin	¼ cup fresh lemon juice
1 cup very hot soy milk or dairy milk	1 teaspoon grated lemon rind
1 cup soft tofu	1 can prepared fruit pie filling (optional)
1 cup creamed cottage cheese	1 cup whipping cream (optional)

Prebake a crumb crust in an 8- or 9-inch springform pan (see page 160). Combine the gelatin with the milk, stirring until gelatin is completely dissolved. Combine with tofu, cottage cheese, salt, lemon juice and rind and the gelatin mixture in a blender or food processor and beat until very smooth. Refrigerate until set.

When set, whip the filling with a rotary beater until it is frothy and light. If it is too stiff, add more water (up to ½ cup). Pour into the prepared crust. Top with canned pie filling or slices of fresh fruit. Serve as is or with whipped cream.

CHEESE-FILLED KRINGLE

Serves 8 to 10

Yeast Dough

1 package (1 tablespoon) active dry yeast	¼ cup oil
¼ cup warm water	3 tablespoons buttermilk or yogurt
¼ cup plus 1 teaspoon sugar	¼ teaspoon salt
⅓ cup soft tofu	1½ cups flour

Combine the yeast with the warm water and 1 teaspoon sugar. (Be sure it foams to show that it is live.)

Combine the tofu, ¼ cup sugar, oil, buttermilk, and salt in a blender or food processor and process until very smooth. Add the yeast mixture. Transfer to a mixing bowl and beat in the flour with a rotary beater, or, if you are using a food processor, add the flour to its bowl. Beat until the dough becomes very elastic.

Cover and let rise until doubled in bulk. You can also put the dough in the refrigerator overnight.

Roll the dough on a floured cloth to a ¼-inch thickness. Line a deep 8- to 10-inch greased cake pan and drape the dough in the pan, letting the excess hang over the sides. Let it rest while you prepare the filling.

Cheese Filling

2 ounces Cheddar cheese (2 1-inch cubes)	1 tablespoon lemon juice
⅓ cup sugar	1 teaspoon vanilla
1 egg	1 cup soft tofu
¼ cup oil	¼ cup raisins
¼ cup flour	1 cup confectioners' sugar
½ teaspoon salt	1 to 2 tablespoons water

Combine the cheese, sugar, egg, oil, flour, salt, lemon juice, and vanilla in a blender or food processor and blend until the cheese is pureed. Add the tofu and beat again. Stir in the raisins.

Making the Kringle

Pour the filling into the dough and fold the excess over the filling. Cover and allow to rise in a warm place for about 1 hour. Preheat oven to 350°F. Bake for about 30 minutes, or until a knife blade comes out clean.

Remove to a rack and glaze while hot with the confectioners' sugar mixed with the water. Cool and serve at room temperature. Store in the refrigerator.

PIES

BANANA CREAM PIE

Serves 6 to 8

1 8- or 9-inch pie shell	2 tablespoons butter
2 tablespoons cornstarch	¼ teaspoon salt
½ cup sugar	1½ cups soft tofu
1 cup cold soy milk or dairy milk	1 teaspoon vanilla
	1 or 2 ripe bananas, sliced

Prebake an 8- or 9-inch pie shell (see page 157). Combine the cornstarch and sugar and dissolve in the milk. Bring to a simmer over medium heat, stirring constantly, until the mixture thickens. Remove from heat and stir in the butter.

Combine the salt, tofu, vanilla, and the cornstarch mixture in a blender or food processor and process until very smooth.

Cool the custard to room temperature. Line the crust with sliced bananas and pour the custard over them. Chill for several hours before serving, either plain or with whipped cream.

CHESS PIE

Serves 6 to 8

⅓ cup water	1 tablespoon oil
1 cup soft tofu	1 cup chopped walnuts or
2 tablespoons flour	pecans
⅓ cup sugar	1 cup raisins
1 teaspoon vanilla	1 (8-inch) unbaked pie
¼ teaspoon salt	shell (see page 157)

Preheat oven to 350°F. Combine the water, tofu, flour, sugar, vanilla, salt, and oil in a blender or food processor and blend until very smooth. Transfer to a bowl and stir in the nuts and raisins. Pour into the pie shell. Bake for 40 minutes, or until a knife inserted in the center comes out clean. Serve warm or cold.

PUMPKIN PIE

Serves 8

Preheat oven to 400°F. Prepare a single crust (see page 157) in a 9- or 10-inch pie pan and prebake for just 7 minutes. Remove to a rack to cool. Reduce oven temperature to 350°F.

Filling

1 cup soft tofu	1 egg (optional)
1½ cups cooked pumpkin	2 to 3 teaspoons pumpkin
½ cup sugar	pie spice, or to taste
2 tablespoons cornstarch	½ teaspoon salt
½ cup milk	

Combine the filling ingredients in a blender jar or food processor bowl and blend until very smooth. Taste and correct flavor.

Pour into the pie shell and bake at 350°F. for 1 hour, or until a knife blade inserted in the center comes out *almost* clean. Cool on a rack and serve at room temperature.

COCONUT CREAM PIE

Coconut Crust   Serves 6 to 8

⅓ cup shredded coconut	1 tablespoon honey
⅓ cup Grape-Nuts® cereal	4 tablespoons melted
⅓ cup crumbs	butter or margarine

Preheat oven to 350°F. Combine the coconut, cereal, and crumbs in a blender jar and blend into fine crumbs. Dribble in the honey while the blender is running. Add the butter in the same way, stopping to scrape down the sides.

Transfer the crumb mixture to a 9-inch pie pan and pat over the bottom and up the sides. Bake for 8 minutes. Cool on a rack before filling. Leave the oven on.

Filling

1 cup coconut flakes	2 tablespoons butter
2 tablespoons cornstarch	⅛ teaspoon salt
½ cup sugar	1½ cups soft tofu
1 cup cold milk	2 teaspoons vanilla

Spread the coconut on a cookie sheet and toast in a 350°F. oven for 5 minutes. Remove and cool.

Combine cornstarch and sugar and stir into the milk. Over medium heat, bring the milk mixture to a boil, stirring constantly, until it becomes quite thick. Add the butter, stirring until it melts.

Blend the salt, tofu, vanilla, and the milk-cornstarch mixture in a food processor or blender. Stir in the coconut and pour into the pie shell. Chill for several hours before serving.

LEMON CUSTARD PIE

Serves 6 to 8

¾ cup sugar
¼ cup all-purpose flour
1½ cups water
2 eggs, separated
¾ cup soft tofu
½ cup lemon juice

2 teaspoons lemon rind
¼ teaspoon salt
1 cup whipping cream
1 8-inch pie prebaked shell (see page 157)

Combine the sugar and flour in a saucepan. Beat the water and egg yolks together and then beat into the sugar-flour mixture. Cook over medium heat, stirring constantly, until the mixture thickens.

Combine the tofu, lemon juice and rind, and salt in a blender or food processor and beat until smooth. Add the hot mixture and blend well. Cool in a cold water bath or in the refrigerator.

Beat the egg whites until very stiff. Fold into the lemon custard and pour into the baked pie shell. Refrigerate until ready for serving. Top with whipped cream.

QUICK YOGURT PIE

Serves 6 to 8

1 cup plain yogurt
1 cup soft tofu
½ cup confectioners' sugar
1 tablespoon lemon juice

1 teaspoon grated lemon rind
¼ teaspoon salt
1 can pie filling (any kind)

Prebake a 9-inch pie shell (see page 157). Combine the yogurt, tofu, sugar, lemon juice and rind and salt in a blender jar or food processor and blend until very smooth. Pour into the prepared pie shell. Top with the pie filling. Chill for several hours before serving.

CRUSTS FOR PIES, FILLED PASTRIES, AND QUICHES

CRUSTS FOR PIES, FILLED PASTRIES, AND QUICHES

1. Short Pastry for Desserts   **1 single crust**

1¼ cups all-purpose flour	½ cup solid shortening
¼ teaspoon baking powder	¼ cup ice water
¼ teaspoon salt	

Preheat oven to 350°F. Mix the flour, baking powder, and salt together. Cut in the shortening with two knives or a pastry blender. If you are using a food processor, use the steel blade and have the shortening as cold as possible.

When mixture is like a very coarse meal, make a well in the center and pour in water. Add water to food processor through feed tube while the machine is running.

Mix in the water very rapidly, stirring until the pastry forms a ball. If this does not happen, add more water by drops.

Refrigerate for about 15 minutes before rolling out. Toss on a well-floured cloth or sheet of waxed paper. Roll out to a circle for an 8, 9, or 10-inch pie pan. (A sheet of waxed paper *over* the pastry helps keep it from sticking to the rolling pin.)

Fold the pastry in half and then into quarters and lift into the pan. It should hang over the edges. Pinch the excess pastry between thumb and forefinger to form a neat, high edge.

Pierce the bottom and sides with a fork to prevent the crust from bubbling and becoming deformed. You can also spread foil over the unbaked crust and fill with dried beans or special metal beads sold for just this purpose.

Bake the shell for 10 minutes, or until it just begins to show a slight brown color. Cool on a rack.

2. Short Pastry for Double Crust

For a double crust, simply double all the amounts in the

above recipe. If you are using a food processor, however, make two single crusts in two separate operations.

When rolling out for a double crust, use three-fifths of the dough for the bottom and two-fifths for the top.

3. Flaky Pastry for Main Courses

2 single or 1 double crust

2¼ cups all-purpose flour	¾ cup cold solid shortening
½ teaspoon salt	

Follow directions for crust 1. This crust is suitable for turnovers, Cornish pasties, quiches, and other main-dish filled pastries.

4. Nut pastry

1 single crust

1 cup cake flour	½ cup butter or other
2 teaspoons sugar	shortening
¼ teaspoon salt	¼ cup ice water
⅓ cup finely ground nuts	

Follow directions for crust 1 (see page 157).

5. Cookie dough for pies

1 single crust

¼ cup sugar	¼ cup soft tofu, or 1 whole
1¼ cups flour	egg
½ teaspoon baking powder	¼ cup cold soy milk or
¼ teaspoon salt	dairy milk
1 tablespoon melted butter or oil	

Mix the sugar, flour, baking powder, and salt together. Beat the butter, tofu, and milk together and add the dry ingredients. If the mixture is too dry, add a bit more milk. Knead for just 10 strokes.

Roll the dough to a ¼-inch thickness and line any shape pan. To prebake, pierce with a fork and bake in a preheated 350°F. oven for 10 to 15 minutes.

**6. Muerbe Teig for Open Pies
or Filled Tortes**   1 (8-inch) square

1 cup flour	¼ cup tofu
1 tablespoon sugar	Milk
½ cup butter or solid shortening, at room temperature	

Mix the flour and sugar together. Combine the butter and tofu and then mix with the flour with a pastry knife or process in a food processor. Add drops of milk to help it come together.

This type of pastry is not rolled out, but patted and pressed into the pan with the fingers to about a quarter of an inch thickness.

7. Whole-Wheat or other Flour Pastry

Substitute any flour or any combination of flours for the amounts called for in the above recipes. If necessary, use more water or milk to hold the dough together. And a word of *caution:* tough crusts are caused by too much liquid, so use only the amount you need to get a workable dough.

CRUMB SHELLS FOR PIES OR QUICHES

1. Graham Cracker Crust   1 (8- to 9-inch) shell

1 cup crushed graham crackers	¼ cup melted butter or margarine
2 tablespoons sugar	

Combine the crumbs and sugar. Blend in the butter with a fork. Spread, pressing in an 8- or 9-inch pie pan or springform pan, covering the bottom with about ¼ inch of the mixture and as much of the sides as possible.

Bake in a preheated 350°F. oven for 10 minutes. Allow to cool before filling.

The crust can also be used without baking. Pat very firmly into the pie pan and refrigerate for several hours before filling.

2. Cookie Crumb Shell   1 single shell

1½ cups crushed cookies   ⅓ cup melted butter or
  (any crisp cookie will do)   margarine

Mix the cookie crumbs and butter with a fork. Spread in a
pie pan and press with a fork or with the fingers.

Bake in a preheated 350°F. oven for 10 minutes. Cool
on a rack before filling.

3. Dry Cereal Shell   2 (9-inch) shells
                                                 or 1 large springform

2 cups crushed dry cereal   ½ teaspoon cinnamon
  (corn, wheat, oat flakes;   ¼ cup white or brown
  Grape-Nuts®; bran   sugar
  flakes, or any   ½ cup melted butter or
  combination of cereal   margarine
  crumbs)

Combine the crumbs, cinnamon, and sugar together and
add the melted butter. Blend well with a fork or with your
fingers. Pat into a pie pan or springform pan and bake in a
preheated 350°F. oven for about 10 minutes, or until the
crust begins to brown. Cool before filling.

This crust may also be used without baking, but it must
be refrigerated for several hours before being filled.

Dry cereal crust is especially good for cheesecakes.
Reserve about one-fourth of the mixture to sprinkle on
top.

4. Crumb Crust for Quiche   1 (8- to 10-inch) shell

1 cup dry bread crumbs   ¼ teaspoon salt
¼ cup unprocessed bran   1 tablespoon dried parsley
¼ cup grated Parmesan,   flakes
  Romano, or other dry   ¼ cup melted butter or
  cheese   margarine

Combine the bread crumbs, bran, cheese, salt, and parsley. Add the melted butter and blend thoroughly. Pat over
the bottom and sides of a pie or quiche pan. Bake in a
preheated 350°F. oven for 10 minutes. Allow to cool
before filling.

PUDDINGS

Puddings go under many names. Whatever they are called: mousse, whip, fromage, or fluff, they are all just delightful when made with tofu.

APRICOT WHIP

Serves 6 to 8

1 cup boiling water
1 envelope (1 tablespoon) unflavored gelatin
2 cups soft tofu
1 cup unsweetened apricot puree
½ cup sugar

1 teaspoon vanilla
¼ teaspoon cinnamon (optional)
2 tablespoons lemon juice
¼ to ½ cup water, soy milk, or dairy milk

Pour the boiling water over the gelatin and stir until the gelatin is completely dissolved. Combine the gelatin mixture, tofu, apricot puree, sugar, vanilla, cinnamon, and lemon juice, in a blender jar or food processor bowl and blend until very smooth. If it is too thick, add just enough water or milk so the mixture blends easily.

Pour the mixture into a bowl and refrigerate until set. Whip with a rotary beater until frothy and light. Pour into individual serving dishes or a glass bowl and refrigerate for an hour or so before serving.

RICH VANILLA PUDDING

Serves 6

2 tablespoons cornstarch	1½ cups soft tofu
1 cup cold soy milk or dairy milk	2 teaspoons vanilla
⅓ cup sugar	Crushed fruit, jam, and/or whipped cream
¼ teaspoon salt	
½ cup soy milk or dairy milk	

Mix the cornstarch and the cold milk together, being sure the cornstarch is completely dissolved. Add the sugar and salt, and cook over medium heat, stirring constantly, until thickened.

Combine the milk, tofu and vanilla in a blender and whip until very smooth. Add the hot cornstarch mixture while mixing at medium speed. Blend well.

Pour into a serving bowl or into individual serving dishes and chill. Serve with fruit, jam, whipped cream or any other garnish you like.

CHESTNUT WHIP

Serves 6

1 envelope (1 tablespoon) unflavored gelatin	1 cup soft tofu
1 cup boiling water	¼ teaspoon salt
1 cup canned chestnut spread (crème de marrons)	2 tablespoons brandy, cognac or coffee liqueur
	½ cup whipping cream (optional)

Dissolve the gelatin in the boiling water. Combine the chestnut spread, tofu, salt, liqueur, and the gelatin mixture in a blender jar or food processor bowl and blend until very smooth. Refrigerate and allow to set.

Whip the cream with a rotary beater and set aside. Then whip the chestnut mixture, with the same beater, until light and frothy. Fold in the whipped cream and pour into individual serving dishes (tall wineglasses are very elegant). Garnish with a fresh leaf from the garden—mint or a rose leaf or petal. Serve immediately or chill again for an hour or two.

If you are not using cream, whip the chestnut mix and serve in the same way.

RASPBERRY WHIP

Serves 6

1 envelope (1 tablespoon) unflavored gelatin	1 10-ounce package frozen raspberries, thawed
1 cup cranberry juice	2 tablespoons lemon juice
¼ cup sugar	½ cup soft tofu

Soften the gelatin in the cranberry juice in a saucepan. Add the sugar and cook over medium heat until the gelatin and sugar are completely dissolved.

Strain the raspberries and reserve the juice. Set the berries aside. Blend the raspberry juice, lemon juice, and the cranberry mixture. Add enough water to measure 2 cups. Then divide juice into two parts. Mix 1 cup with the raspberries and pour into a glass serving bowl or a fancy 1½-quart mold.

Combine the second cup of juice with the tofu in the blender and whip very smooth. Refrigerate in a separate bowl.

When the tofu is set, whip with a rotary beater at high speed until it is light and frothy. Pour over the raspberry mold. Chill until set.

Serve with raspberry or vanilla flavored yogurt, or whipped cream.

CRANBERRY MOUSSE

Serves 8

1 envelope (1 tablespoon) unflavored gelatin
¾ cup water
½ cup sugar
⅛ teaspoon salt
1 teaspoon grated orange rind

¾ cup soft tofu
1½ cups whole fresh cranberries
2 egg whites (optional)

Combine the gelatin, water, sugar, and salt in a saucepan and cook until the sugar and gelatin are completely dissolved.

Combine the orange rind and tofu in a blender jar or food processor bowl with enough of the gelatin mixture to make blending easy. Blend at high speed until smooth. Add the cranberries and process until they are chopped very fine. Add the remaining gelatin mixture to the blender or pour into a separate bowl and stir together. Refrigerate until set.

Beat egg whites until very stiff. Beat the jelled cranberry mixture until frothy, then fold in the egg whites.

Serve as a mousse or a torte. For a torte, pour into a springform pan that has been lined with a crumb crust and prebaked (see page 160). Refrigerate for several hours and garnish with slices of orange before serving.

For a mousse, pour the mixture into a glass bowl or into individual serving glasses. Refrigerate for several hours or overnight.

MANDARIN MOUSSE

Serves 8

1 envelope (1 tablespoon)
unflavored gelatin
⅓ cup cold water
1 cup soy milk or dairy
milk
¼ teaspoon salt
1 cup soft tofu
½ cup orange juice

1 teaspoon grated orange
rind
½ cup sugar
¼ cup cocoa
2 teaspoons vanilla
Whipping cream
(optional)

Soften the gelatin in the cold water. Heat the milk to scalding. Add the salt and the gelatin and stir until the gelatin is dissolved.

Combine the tofu, orange juice and rind, sugar, cocoa, vanilla, and gelatin mixture in a blender or food processor bowl and blend until very smooth. Pour into a bowl and refrigerate until set.

If you are using the cream, whip it with a rotary beater until fairly stiff, then whip the orange-cocoa mixture with the same beater until frothy and light. Fold in the whipped cream. Spoon into individual serving glasses or into a mold and refrigerate for several hours or overnight before serving.

COFFEE LIQUEUR MOUSSE

Serves 6

1 envelope (1 tablespoon)
unflavored gelatin
½ cup cold coffee
1 cup soy milk or dairy
milk
⅓ cup sugar
4 teaspoons instant coffee
2 eggs, separated

⅛ teaspoon salt
1 cup soft tofu
¼ cup Kahlúa, Tia Maria,
or Sabra
1 teaspoon vanilla
Toasted, slivered
almonds

Soften the gelatin in the cold coffee. Combine the milk, sugar, instant coffee, and egg yolks in a heavy-bottomed saucepan and beat with a wire whisk. Cook over medium heat, stirring constantly, until the mixture begins to thicken. Remove from heat, add the gelatin and stir until it is dissolved. Pour into a blender jar and add the salt, tofu, liqueur, and vanilla. Blend until very smooth. Transfer to another bowl and refrigerate until set.

Beat the egg whites with a rotary beater until stiff. Then beat the set mousse with the beater until light and frothy. Fold the egg whites into the mousse. Pour into serving dishes and refrigerate overnight. Top with toasted, slivered almonds.

ORANGE MOUSSE

Serves 6

1 envelope (1 tablespoon) gelatin
½ cup cold water
1 cup very hot orange juice
¼ cup sugar
1 teaspoon grated orange rind

1 cup soft tofu
¼ cup orange liqueur
1 cup canned mandarin oranges, drained, or 1 cup fresh orange segments

Soften the gelatin in the cold water. Blend with the orange juice and stir until the gelatin is dissolved. Combine the orange mixture with the sugar, orange rind, tofu, and liqueur in a blender and process until very smooth. Pour into a bowl and refrigerate until set.

When set, beat with a rotary beater until light and frothy. Spoon into a glass serving bowl or individual stem glasses in layers of mousse and orange segments. Refrigerate for several hours or overnight before serving.

CITRON FROMAGE (Lemon Fluff)

Serves 10

1 envelope (1 tablespoon) unflavored gelatin	2 eggs, separated
½ cup cold water	1 cup soft tofu
¾ cup sugar	2 teaspoons grated lemon rind
1½ cups water	½ cup lemon juice, to taste
¼ teaspoon salt	

Soften the gelatin in the cold water. Combine the sugar, water, and salt in a saucepan and bring to a simmer. Add the gelatin mixture and cook, stirring, until the gelatin is dissolved. Beat the egg yolks into the hot mixture very quickly and cook for a minute or two until it begins to thicken.

In a blender or food processor, process the tofu, lemon rind, and lemon juice together. Add the gelatin mixture and blend until very smooth. Taste and correct for sweetness or tartness. Pour into a bowl and refrigerate until set.

Whip the egg whites with a rotary beater until stiff. Beat the set lemon mixture with the beater until light and frothy. Fold in the egg whites. Spoon into a serving dish or mold or into individual serving dishes and refrigerate for several hours or overnight before serving.

PUMPKIN OR SQUASH CHIFFON PUDDING

Serves 6

¾ cup water	1 teaspoon pumpkin pie spice
⅔ cup brown sugar	¼ teaspoon salt
1 envelope (1 tablespoon) unflavored gelatin	1 teaspoon vanilla
1 cup soft tofu	2 tablespoons brandy (optional)
1 cup cooked pumpkin or yellow squash	

Bring water and sugar to a boil. Add the gelatin and stir until sugar and gelatin are dissolved. Remove from heat.

Combine tofu, pumpkin, spice, salt, vanilla, and brandy

in a blender or food processor and add the gelatin mixture while the machine is still running. Blend until very smooth. Pour into a bowl and refrigerate until set. Whip with a rotary beater until light and frothy. Pour into a prebaked pie shell of your choice (see pages 157 to 160) or individual serving glasses. Refrigerate for several hours.

CAKES

LEMON YOGURT CAKE

Serves 9–10

4 tablespoons butter or margarine
½ cup sugar
⅓ cup soft tofu
1 tablespoon water
¼ teaspoon salt
½ cup yogurt
1 teaspoon grated lemon rind
1 tablespoon lemon juice
½ teaspoon baking soda
1¼ cups all-purpose flour

Preheat oven to 350°F. Grease an 8- by 8-inch cake pan. Beat butter and sugar together in a food processor or with a rotary beater. Add the tofu, water, and salt and beat well. Add the yogurt, lemon rind and juice, and soda and beat until light and creamy. Add all the flour at once and mix only lightly until it is moistened.

Spoon into the prepared pan and bake for 40 to 50 minutes, or until a toothpick inserted in the middle comes out clean. Cool on a rack. Serve with whipped cream or honey syrup.

Honey Syrup

½ cup honey
¾ cup water
¼ teaspoon grated lemon rind
2 teaspoons lemon juice

Combine the ingredients in a saucepan and bring to a boil. Reduce heat and simmer, uncovered, for about 10 minutes.

When the cake has been out of the oven for about 5 minutes, pierce the surface all over with a fork or a skewer and spoon the syrup over the hot cake. Cool to room temperature before serving. Unsweetened whipped cream is wonderful with the honey-soaked cake.

FUDGE TORTE

1 layer

2 teaspoons instant coffee
¼ cup water
6 ounces (1 cup) semisweet chocolate chips
¼ cup plus 1 tablespoon butter
¾ cup soft tofu

¼ cup water
¼ teaspoon salt
½ teaspoon almond extract
⅓ cup okara or almond paste
¼ teaspoon baking soda
1 teaspoon baking powder
¾ cup all-purpose flour

Preheat oven to 350°F. Grease an 8-inch layer cake or springform pan. Combine the coffee, water, ⅔ cup of the chocolate chips, and the ¼ cup butter in a saucepan and cook over low heat until melted and smooth. Remove from heat. Combine with tofu, water, salt, almond extract, okara, soda, and baking powder in a food processor or mixing bowl and beat well. To this, add the chocolate mixture and beat again. Stir in the flour and mix until flour is moistened.

Spread in the prepared pan and bake for 30 minutes (do not overbake). Cool on a rack for 10 minutes, then turn out and replace on rack to cool completely. When the torte is cool, glaze with ⅓ cup chocolate chips melted with the 1 tablespoon butter. Serve at room temperature.

CHOCOLATE APPLESAUCE CAKE

1 large bundt cake

⅔ cup oil
8 ounces (1⅓ cups) chocolate chips, or ⅔ cup cocoa
½ cup sugar (1 cup sugar, if you use cocoa)
1 cup soft tofu
2 cups applesauce
½ teaspoon salt
¼ teaspoon ground cloves

2 teaspoon baking soda
2 teaspoon cream of tartar
2 teaspoons vanilla
3 tablespoons cornstarch
3 cups all-purpose flour
1 to 2 cups raisins (optional)
1 cup chopped nuts (any kind)
Confectioners' sugar

Preheat oven to 350°F. Combine the oil, chocolate chips, sugar, tofu, applesauce, salt, cloves, soda, cream of tartar, vanilla, and cornstarch in the bowl of a food processor or in a mixing bowl. Mix well. (The chocolate chips should be cut into small pieces.) Add the flour all at once and mix only until it is moistened. Stir in the raisins and nuts.

Spoon into a well-oiled bundt pan, or large tube pan. Bake for about 1 hour, or until the cake springs back when touched and begins to leave the sides of the pan. Cool on a rack for 10 minutes, then turn out on a plate and dust with confectioners' sugar while still warm.

YOGURT FLAN

Serves 6 to 8

1 cup plain yogurt
1¼ cups soft tofu
1½ tablespoons cornstarch
2 eggs
¼ cup salad oil
⅓ cup sugar
2 teaspoons vanilla extract
½ teaspoon grated lemon rind

¼ teaspoon salt
A dash of ground cloves
Soy milk or dairy milk to thin
1 9-inch unbaked pie shell (see pages 157 to 160)

Preheat oven to 425°F. Combine all the ingredients but the milk in a blender or food processor bowl and beat until very smooth. If it is too thick, add a spoonful or two of milk. Pour into the unbaked pie shell and bake for 10 minutes. While it is baking prepare the topping:

Topping

¼ cup brown sugar

⅓ cup chopped nuts

¼ teaspoon cinnamon

Combine the ingredients and sprinkle over the partly baked flan. Reduce oven heat to 350°F. and continue baking for about 30 to 40 minutes, or until a knife blade comes out *almost* clean. Cool on a rack and serve either lukewarm or chilled.

CHOCOLATE RAISIN BARS

About 15 bars

4 tablespoons melted shortening or oil

⅓ cup cocoa

1 teaspoon vanilla

3 tablespoons buttermilk or soured milk

½ cup soft tofu

½ cup unprocessed bran or okara

½ cup sugar

½ teaspoon salt

1 teaspoon baking powder

¾ cup flour

½ to 1 cup raisins

Preheat oven to 350°F. Grease an 11- by 17-inch pan. Combine the shortening and cocoa in a blender jar or food processor bowl and beat until smooth. Add the vanilla, buttermilk, and tofu and blend again. Transfer the mixture to a bowl and add the bran.

Mix the sugar, salt, baking powder, and flour in a separate bowl. Combine with the tofu mixture and stir together quickly. Add the raisins. If you don't like raisins, use nuts instead—or don't use anything.

Spread in prepared pan and bake for no more than 20 minutes. Cool on a rack in the pan. Cut into squares.

BAKED FUDGE BROWNIES

20 (2-inch) squares

⅓ cup cocoa
2 tablespoons oil or melted butter
½ cup soft tofu
1 teaspoon vanilla
¼ cup unprocessed bran or okara

⅔ cup sugar
½ teaspoon baking powder
¼ teaspoon salt
⅓ cup flour
½ cup chopped nuts

Preheat oven to 350°F. Grease an 8- by 10-inch pan. Combine the cocoa, oil, tofu, and vanilla in a mixing bowl and beat well. Add the bran, sugar, baking powder, salt, and flour and stir together quickly. If the mixture is too thick, add a few drops of water. Stir in the nuts. Spread in the prepared pan and bake for no more than 20 minutes. Cool on a rack in the pan then cut into squares.

DANISH PASTRY

2 large coffee cakes or 12 to 20 individual Danish pastries

2 packages (2 tablespoons) active dry yeast
½ cup warm water
¼ cup plus 1 teaspoon sugar
1 egg (optional)
¾ cup soft tofu

½ cup buttermilk
½ cup okara (optional)
½ teaspoon baking soda
½ cup melted butter or margarine
½ teaspoon salt
4 to 5 cups flour

Prove the yeast by combining with the water and the 1 teaspoon sugar; if live, it will foam up in a few minutes.

Combine the egg, tofu, the ¼ cup sugar, buttermilk, okara, soda, butter, and salt in a blender and beat until smooth. Add the yeast mixture and beat again.

Pour into a mixing bowl and add about 1½ cups flour. Beat very well before adding more flour. When the dough becomes too thick to beat, transfer to a floured board and knead in enough flour to make an elastic, shiny dough.

Place in an oiled bowl, cover and let rise for 2 hours or refrigerate overnight.

When ready to bake, punch the dough down and transfer to a floured board. Knead the dough briefly and divide for different kinds of pastry. Try the following variations.

1. Caramel Buns   12 buns

Topping

3 tablespoons butter	½ cup chopped or whole
½ cup brown sugar	walnuts or pecans
2 tablespoons water	

Melt the butter in a heavy 10- to 12-inch skillet. Sprinkle with brown sugar and water. Cook, stirring for 1 minute. Spread the nuts over the sugar mix and leave in the skillet.

Assembling the Caramel Buns

Roll out half of the Danish Pastry dough to an oval about 12 by 18 inches. Brush with melted butter and sprinkle with cinnamon, raisins, and sugar. Roll the dough up lengthwise. Cut the roll into slices about 1½ inches thick and arrange, cut side down, over the nuts and caramel mixture in the skillet. The slices do not need to be touching as they will expand while they rise.

Cover and let rise until double in bulk. Preheat the oven to 350°F. while the pastry rises. Bake for 30 to 40 minutes, or until they are nicely browned and sound hollow when tapped. Place a large plate over the pastry and flip the skillet over. Let the buns stand on the plate for about 5 minutes with the skillet over it like a cap. Remove the skillet and scrape out any caramel remaining on the bottom and spread it on the pastry.

2. Tofu-Filled Pastry   1 large pastry

Filling

¼ cup melted butter
¼ to ½ cup raisins
   Cinnamon

½ cup sugar
8 (¼-inch) slices of soft
   tofu

Assembling the pastry

Roll out half of the Danish Pastry recipe into a long oval about 12 inches by 18 inches. Brush with melted butter. Sprinkle with raisins, cinnamon, and half the sugar. Arrange 2 rows of tofu slices along the length of the oval. Sprinkle with more cinnamon and the remaining sugar. Roll up lengthwise and pinch edges shut. Arrange on a cookie sheet in a circle or pretzel shape or any shape that is pleasing to you.

Cover and let rise until doubled in size. Preheat the oven to 350°F. while the pastry rises. Bake 15 to 25 minutes, or until nicely browned. Remove to a rack to cool. If you wish to frost the pastry, use the following glaze:

Powdered Sugar Glaze

1 cup powdered
   (confectioners') sugar

1 tablespoon very hot
   water

Mix the sugar and water, adding more hot water if needed. Pour this over the hot or very warm pastry. Confectioners' sugar contains cornstarch and the heat of the cake will "cook" the frosting.

3. Fruit filled Individual Pastries   6 to 8 pastries

Filling

¼ to ⅓ cup melted butter or
   margarine
1 cup of any of the
   following:
      apricot jam, preserves
   or puree
      strawberry jam,
   preserves or puree
      raspberry jam,
   preserves or puree
      prune puree

Assembling the pastries:

Roll out half the Danish Pastry dough into a long oval
about ¼-inch thick. Cut this into 4- to 5-inch squares.
Brush each with melted butter and then fill the centers
with 1 to 2 tablespoons of one of the fruit preparations.

Pull the corners of the each square toward the center
and pinch the seams to keep the pastry from opening.
Place on a baking sheet, cover, and let rise until doubled
in size. Preheat the oven to 350°F. while the pastries rise.
Bake about 15 or 20 minutes, or until nicely browned.
Glaze with powdered sugar glaze (see page 174) while still
hot.

4. Plain Kringle

Filling

⅓ cup melted butter or
   margarine
½ cup brown sugar,
   granulated sugar or
   honey
   Cinnamon to taste
¼ to ½ cup raisins

½ to 1 cup chopped
   walnuts or pecans
1 egg white
2 teaspoons water
¼ to ½ cup granulated
   sugar

Roll out half the Danish Pastry dough into an oval about
12 inches by 18 inches and ¼-inch thick. Brush with melted

butter. Sprinkle with sugar, cinnamon, raisins, and half the nuts.

Form into a long roll. Make the roll longer by squeezing and pulling it with your hands. Transfer to a baking sheet and form into the traditional Kringle, a large pretzel-like shape.

Beat the egg white with the water. Brush the top of the kringle with the egg mixture and sprinkle with sugar and the remaining nuts. Cover with a cloth and place in a draft-free place to rise.

When about doubled in bulk, bake in a preheated 350°F. oven for 25 to 35 minutes, or until nicely browned. Cool on the baking sheet on a rack.

COOKIES

These cookies are made with tofu instead of eggs. I do not think you will be able to tell the difference, except that these are better.

SPRITZ COOKIES

About 5 dozen cookies

1 cup softened butter or margarine	⅓ cup soft tofu
½ cup sugar	½ teaspoon salt
	2½ cups flour

Preheat oven to 400°F. Beat butter until light. Add sugar and blend well. Beat in the tofu and salt. Add enough of the flour to make a soft dough. Force through a cookie press directly onto an ungreased cookie sheet, into any desired shape. Bake from 8 to 10 minutes at 400°F. Cool completely before storing in airtight containers.

OATMEAL CRISPS

48 (2-inch) cookies

½ cup solid shortening	½ teaspoon cinnamon
¼ cup oil	1½ cups flour
¾ cup brown sugar	¼ cup wheat germ
¾ cup granulated sugar	¼ cup Grape-Nuts® cereal
⅓ cup soft tofu	(or other crisp cereal)
1 teaspoon vanilla	1½ cups rolled oats
½ teaspoon salt	½ cup chopped nuts
½ teaspoon baking soda	

Preheat oven to 350°F. Combine the shortening, oil, sugars, tofu, vanilla, salt, soda, and cinnamon in a mixing bowl or food processor. Mix until well blended.

Add the flour, ½ cup at a time, mixing well after each addition (the dough should be a little sticky).

Stir in the wheat germ, cereal, oats, and nuts. Drop by teaspoonfuls on an ungreased cookie sheet. Bake for about 10 minutes. Cool completely before storing in an airtight container.

BROWN SUGAR COOKIES

About 40 cookies

½ cup butter	½ teaspoon baking powder
½ cup brown sugar	¼ teaspoon salt
¼ cup soft tofu	Chopped or whole
2 cups all-purpose flour	almonds or pecans

Preheat oven to 400°F. Beat the butter until fluffy. Add the sugar and beat again, then beat in the tofu. Combine the flour, baking powder, and salt, and then mix with the butter mixture to achieve a smooth dough.

Form into one or two long rolls, about 2 inches in diameter and refrigerate for 30 minutes. (The dough may also be frozen and baked at a later time.)

Cut into ¼-inch slices and arrange on an ungreased cookie sheet. Top each with a whole nut or chopped nuts.

(If you use chopped nuts, press them into the dough with a fork.)

— Bake for 10 to 12 minutes. Cool completely and store in airtight containers.

BUTTER COOKIES

About 60 cookies

1 cup softened butter	2 teaspoons vanilla
½ cup sugar	*or*
¼ cup soft tofu	1 tablespoon brandy
2 teaspoons lemon juice plus ½ teaspoon lemon rind *or*	½ teaspoon baking powder
	3 cups flour

Cream the batter until fluffy, then add the sugar, tofu, flavoring, and baking powder. Work in as much of the flour as the moist mixture will handle. Knead just ten strokes on a floured board. Refrigerate for an hour before using.

Preheat oven to 350°F. before rolling out the cookies.

Roll out dough to less than ¼-inch thick. Cut with cookie cutters, a knife, or the rim of a small glass. Place on ungreased cookie sheets.

To Decorate:

1 egg white	½ cup chopped nuts
¼ cup granulated sugar	

Beat the egg white until frothy and brush on the unbaked cookies. Sprinkle with a mixture of sugar and chopped nuts.

Bake for 10 to 15 minutes. Cool completely before storing.

GINGERSNAPS

About 75 cookies

2 cups sugar
¾ cup softened butter or margarine
½ cup soft tofu
1½ teaspoons baking soda
½ cup molasses
2 teaspoons vinegar
½ teaspoon salt

2 teaspoons ground ginger
Dash of cinnamon, cloves, and nutmeg (to taste)
3½ cups flour
Granulated sugar for topping

Preheat oven to 350°F. Beat the sugar and butter until creamy. Add the tofu, soda, molasses, vinegar, salt, ginger, and other spices. Work in flour until it forms a ball that can be handled easily.

Form into balls the size of a walnut. Place far apart on an ungreased cookie sheet to allow for spreading. Bake for 10 to 12 minutes, or until they begin to show color around the edges. Sprinkle with granulated sugar while hot. Cool and store in an airtight container.

PEANUT BUTTER COOKIES

About 90 cookies

1 cup shortening
¾ cup brown sugar
¾ cup granulated sugar
½ cup soft tofu
1 teaspoon vanilla

1½ teaspoons baking soda
½ teaspoon salt
1 cup peanut butter
3 cups flour

Preheat oven to 400°F. Cream shortening and sugars. Blend in the tofu, vanilla, soda, salt, and peanut butter. Mix until very smooth. Work in as much flour as necessary to make a soft dough.

Roll into balls about ¾ inch in diameter or drop by teaspoonfuls. Place about an inch apart on an ungreased cookie sheet and criss-cross with the tines of a fork. Bake for about 8 minutes. Cool completely before storing in airtight containers.

CARAMEL SQUARES •

About 16 squares

¼ cup butter or margarine
1 cup brown sugar
¼ cup soft tofu
¼ teaspoon salt

½ teaspoon vanilla
1 cup flour
1 teaspoon baking powder
¼ to ½ cup chopped nuts

Preheat oven to 300°F. Grease an 8-inch square baking pan. Melt the butter and sugar together, stirring constantly. Allow to cool. Beat in the tofu, salt, and vanilla. Mix the flour and baking powder and add to tofu mixture. Stir just until flour is moistened. Add the nuts.

Spread in the prepared pan and bake for 20 minutes. Do not overbake; the bars should be chewy. Cut into squares and cool in the pan.

ALMOND ICEBOX COOKIES

About 60 cookies

1 cup softened butter or
   margarine
½ cup brown sugar
½ cup granulated sugar
⅓ cup soft tofu
1 teaspoon baking soda

1 teaspoon cinnamon
½ teaspoon salt
2 to 2½ cups flour
½ to 1 cup whole almonds,
   blanched

Cream the butter and sugars. Add the tofu, soda, cinnamon, and salt. Beat well. Stir in the flour, using only enough to make a firm, moist dough. Work in the almonds.

Form into rolls about 2 inches in diameter, wrap in waxed paper, and place in the freezer until ready to bake.

When ready to bake, preheat the oven to 350°F. With a sharp knife, cut each roll into ¼-inch slices. Arrange on an ungreased baking sheet. Bake for about 8 minutes, or until lightly browned. Cool before storing.

POPPY SEED COOKIES

About 50 cookies

1 cup poppy seeds
½ cup hot soy milk or dairy milk
½ cup butter or margarine, softened
½ cup sugar
¼ cup soft tofu
1 teaspoon vanilla
½ teaspoon salt
⅛ teaspoon dried tarragon leaves, crushed
¼ teaspoon ground cloves
1 teaspoon baking powder
1¼ cups flour
Confectioners' sugar

Preheat oven to 350°F. Soak the poppy seeds in the milk for about 10 minutes. Beat the butter, sugar, tofu, vanilla, salt, tarragon, cloves, and baking powder together in a food processor or mixer. Add the poppy seeds and then the flour. Mix thoroughly. Drop by teaspoonfuls on an ungreased cookie sheet. Bake about 15 to 20 minutes. Sprinkle with confectioners' sugar while still warm. Cool before storing.

SOFT MOLASSES COOKIES

About 48 cookies

This recipe makes excellent gingerbread men or parts for gingerbread houses.

½ cup butter or margarine
½ cup sugar
⅓ cup soft tofu
½ cup molasses
½ cup sour cream
1 teaspoon cinnamon
1 teaspoon ground ginger
½ teaspoon baking soda
½ teaspoon cream of tartar
1½ cups flour
½ to 1 cup raisins (optional)

Preheat oven to 350°F. Beat the butter until soft. Add the sugar and cream well. Then add the tofu, molasses, sour cream, cinnamon, and ginger and blend thoroughly. Mix the soda, cream of tartar and flour together and add to the tofu mixture to form a soft dough. Chill for 1 hour or so.

On a well-floured cloth or board, knead the dough for

about 1 minute. Roll out to a ¼-inch thickness and cut with a cookie cutter or with a knife into large forms. Bake on an ungreased cookie sheet for 15 to 20 minutes. Frost while lukewarm. A simple icing follows.

Icing

1 teaspoon butter	¼ teaspoon vanilla
2 tablespoons hot water, or milk or cream	Drops of food color (optional)
1 cup confectioners' sugar	

Blend the butter with the hot liquid, then add the vanilla and mix. Beat in the sugar until icing is the proper consistency for spreading.

If you wish to color the icing, divide into parts and tint each separately with drops of food color. Spread on tops of lukewarm cookies.

11

BEVERAGES

Tofu is excellent in two delicious and refreshing beverages. Both are as rich and creamy as if they were made with ice cream. They are high in protein, low in calories and have no cholesterol at all, and they are definitely not made with ice cream.

THE TOFU SHAKE

Serves 2

1 cup soft tofu
½ to 1 cup soy milk, milk
   or water
1 teaspoon lemon juice

1 tablespoon sugar or
   honey
1 teaspoon vanilla
Pinch of salt

Combine the tofu, ½ cup of the liquid, lemon juice, sweetener, vanilla, and salt in a blender jar and blend until very smooth. If the shake is too thick, add liquid until it is the desired consistency.

To flavor the basic shake:

Chocolate: Add 3 teaspoons cocoa and a dash of
                cinnamon
Mocha: Add 1½ teaspoons cocoa, 1 teaspoon
                instant coffee and use brewed coffee as
                the liquid instead milk
Coffee: Add 2 teaspoons instant coffee and use
                brewed coffee as the liquid
Vanilla: Add 1½ teaspoons extra vanilla, a bit more
                sweetener and a dash of cinnamon
Strawberry or   Add 2 tablespoons jam or preserves and
Raspberry: no sweetener
Fresh Fruit: Add ½ to 1 cup fruit and adjust sweetening
                to taste

Always taste and correct flavorings. Add liquid to thin, if necessary.

THE TOFU SMOOTHIE

Serves 2

1 cup soft tofu
1 ripe banana
1 tablespoon lemon juice
1 tablespoon sugar or honey

1 teaspoon vanilla
¼ teaspoon salt
Fruit juice, buttermilk, yogurt or water to thin

In a blender jar or food processor bowl, combine the tofu, banana, lemon juice, sweetener, vanilla, salt, and enough liquid to make blending possible. Blend until very smooth.

To Flavor the Basic Smoothie:

Fruit: Add ½ to 1 cup fresh fruit or ½ cup frozen or preserved fruit

Chocolate or   Add 1 tablespoon cocoa or carob, and
Carob: sweeten to taste

Another natural use for tofu in a beverage is in a flavorful concoction formerly made with eggs—indeed what would be Christmas and New Year's without it. It could be called "Tofunog."

EGGNOG (Eggless)

Serves 4

2 cups soft tofu
½ to ¾ cup brandy, rum, or whiskey
⅓ cup sugar, or to taste

2 teaspoons vanilla
¼ teaspoon salt
¼ teaspoon nutmeg
Milk or water to thin

Combine the tofu, liquor, sugar, vanilla, salt, and nutmeg in a blender jar or food processor bowl and blend until very smooth. Add milk, water or more liquor to thin to the desired consistency. Taste and correct flavor.

Chill for several hours before serving. Serve with a dusting of fresh nutmeg.

HIGH PROTEIN BREAKFAST BEVERAGE

Tofu is the perfect base for a nourishing liquid breakfast or high protein diet drink. You can vary the ingredients as you wish.

1 quart

1½ cups soft tofu
 1 cup soy milk, dairy milk or ⅓ cup powdered milk plus ⅔ cup water
 1 to 2 tablespoons vegetable oil
 1 to 2 tablespoons honey, or to taste
 1 or 2 eggs (optional)
 1 or 2 teaspoons vanilla
    Dash of cinnamon

 ½ cup any fruit or ½ banana
 ¼ cup lemon juice
 1 tablespoon liquid or granular lecithin
 1 tablespoon, or more, nutritional yeast or protein powder
 1 tablespoon calcium gluconate
 ¼ cup wheat germ

Combine all the ingredients in the blender jar and process until very smooth. Taste and correct flavoring. Store in the refrigerator.

Nutritional Information:*

	1 Quart	6 ounces
Calories	956	179
Protein (grams)	65.8	12.4
Carbohydrates (grams)	84	15.6
Fat (grams)	46.7	8.7

* These figures do not include the nutritional yeast or protein supplement.

AN AFTERWORD

Now the writing is over, the recipe testing is ended for a while, and the stove is temporarily cold. I look back and marvel at five years of exploration into the marvels of tofu and know that this pause is only temporary. There is still more to know, still more to explore.

It isn't easy to be a pioneer, but I find it's lots of fun. That is why I do it. I am not, by nature, a proselytizer or an altruist. I distrust those who say they are. I have done all this cooking for myself, my family, my friends and anyone else who might be interested. If my enthusiasm for tofu rubs off on a few passersby, they will be better for it.

I won't force Vernon, my neighbor across the street, to eat tofu if he doesn't want to. I can't get mad at him or at Bill, the butcher, because they haven't seen the same star I have. That is their problem. And yours, too, if that's how you are.

My patience is a little tested by people like the lady at the auto license office who handed me my California Environmental plates which spell: TO TOFU.

"What's that mean?" she asked. I told her that tofu is that white, custardy stuff you get in Chinese restaurants.

"Yuk," she said. "I wouldn't put that in my mouth!"

I meet that sort of attitude almost every day, but I'm not discouraged, because I was the same way at one time. I remember practicing my chopsticks technique by picking little cubes of tofu out of the food and setting them on the edge of the plate.

But the attitudes of many are changing, and in some very gratifying ways.

There are the 62 letters I got from people in and around Columbus, Ohio, because of a mixup in a Cook's Corner column. They all wanted tofu recipes and some wrote warm personal notes about their experiences with tofu.

There was the tofu-making class in Marin County, California, last year. The class was limited to 30 people but 36 people came, and there was a waiting list of 36 more.

There is the warm feeling I get when I am greeted by a car full of Chinese or Japanese people who have speeded up to pass me just to see who is driving the car with the "TO TOFU" license plate.

There are the smiles of amusement on the faces of natives of Japantown in San Jose, California, when I am shopping at the tofu store and buy a huge amount of okara to feed my dog. (Yes, his name is Tofu.)

All this—and more, makes the whole thing worth while.

And where do the recipes come from? I am asked. Right out of here (I am pointing to my head) and there (a sweeping gesture at a bookshelf full of cookbooks). And after a little experience you can do it, too. It is nothing more than learning the nature of the stuff and plugging it into your favorite recipes. I hope that you will find wonder and excitement in cooking with tofu the way I have.

Juel Andersen

APPENDIX 1

PROTEIN AND
PROTEIN COMPLEMENTARITY

". . . oats, peas, beans, and barley, too . . ." is an old refrain from my childhood. I don't remember what it meant then, but *now* it becomes a way to remember to include these foods in a list that has long excluded them—that of protein foods. While you are adding to the list, which all of us know includes meat, fish, poultry, eggs, and dairy products, add: wheat, rice, corn, and every other food you can think of.

What is the meaning of such a list? Simply that every food we eat contains *some* protein, and that protein comes in two varieties: animal and vegetable. Protein is the very stuff of life; it is needed for the formation and the replenishment of bones, skin, muscles, hair, blood, nails . . . in fact, all body tissues. Our bodies don't care *what* the source of the protein is; they care very much that there is enough and that it is the right kind.

There are 22 proteins or amino acids needed by the body. Most of these can be made by our bodies from raw materials supplied by the foods we eat. The important ones that cannot be synthesized are called the "essential amino acids." These are: isoleucine, leucine, lysine, cystine/methionine (sulphur-containing), threonine, tryptophan, valine, phenylalanine/tyrosine (aromatic), and histidine.

The word *essential* means that these amino acids are:
1. *essential* in human diet.
2. *essential* that we get these in the foods we eat.
3. *essential* that all be present in the body at the same time.
4. *essential* that they be present in the right proportions.

Most foods are limited in one or more of the essential

amino acids, even our most honored protein foods. Steak and roast beef have marginal amounts of tryptophan, which wheat has in more than adequate supply. (It is curious that we are accustomed to eating meat and bread together.) The protein in beef is complete since it does contain all the essential proteins, but eating wheat with beef enhances the protein array, so that more protein is available to be used by the body. In other words, we get more protein from both the meat and the bread when we eat them together. This is called "complementarity" and it works for all sorts of food combinations. It also means that you get more protein for your money, something extra that is free for the taking.

In many parts of the world people do not eat great quantities of meat and meat products, as we do. Because of economic problems, availability, and often because of religion, grains and legumes become the basic foods. These, in combination with dairy products and seeds, provide ample protein.

Beans and rice are a combination eaten in many lands. The beans are limited in methionine, which is supplied by the rice. The rice is limited in lysine, which is supplied by the beans. Together they form a high-quality complete protein. Grains (oats, wheat, corn, and rice) and legumes (beans, peas, and lentils) complement each other. The quantities of these foods that must be eaten are greater than one would need to get the same amount of protein from animal sources. Adding dairy products greatly increases the protein content of these foods.

Soybeans are the best source of vegetable protein, and they contain all the essential amino acids. They are, however, limited in cystine/methionine (sulphur-containing amino acids), which can be supplied by complementing soyfoods with rice, wheat, eggs, dairy products, other grains and some seeds. By serving soyfoods in combination with one or more of these other foods, the available protein can be increased by as much as 40 percent.

This fact is not lost on the stock farmers. They raise their animals on scientifically quantified feed made up of just such protein-enhancing combinations of soybean and grains.

Complementation is, then, the art of combining protein

foods so that the array of essential amino acids that the body can obtain from these foods will be at the maximum. I say "art" because it is not necessary to make a cult or a science of combining foods, nor is it necessary to be sure to do your combining at the same time or at the same meal. You must become familiar with the basic combinations and see to it that you use a wide variety of foods when preparing meals that use little or no meat.

In this book we are most interested in how to use tofu. Many recipes in this book automatically use other ingredients that complement the soy protein, something that just happens in this kind of cooking.

Table 1 lists foods complementary to tofu. Serving such foods together or within the same day increases the protein that can be used by the body.

Table 1. COMPLEMENTARY FOODS TO SERVE WITH TOFU*

Tofu*	+	Grains: wheat, rye, barley, millet, oats, corn, rice
Tofu	+	Seeds: Sesame, poppy
Tofu	+	Dairy foods: Cheese, cow's milk
Tofu	+	Animal foods: Eggs, chicken
Tofu	+	Legumes: Peanuts, beans, peas
Tofu	+	Seafoods: Shrimp, tuna, cod
Tofu	+	Any combinations of the above

Most Americans eat more protein than is required by the body for its building and rebuilding of tissues. The Recommended Daily Allowance (RDA) for protein is about 56 grams for the average man and 44 grams for the average woman. The actual needs vary more with age and size than with activity.

Many of our beliefs about protein are just not true.

*Okara and soy milk are complemented in the same way.

Eating more protein than you need will not make you stronger. It will actually make you fatter. Strenuous exercise does not require eating extra protein. The energy consumed in exercising can better be supplied by carbohydrates. And while animal protein is of high quality, so is the protein in wheat germ, soybeans and dried yeast.

Table 2 shows the Recommended Daily Allowances for protein. The values are set high to allow for a margin of safety. It has been shown in controlled studies that active men can remain healthy and vigorous eating as little as 30 to 35 grams a day. That amount could be provided by about 5 ounces of Swiss cheese *or* 6 ounces of lean hamburger *or* 10 ounces of soft tofu.

Table 2: RECOMMENDED DAILY PROTEIN ALLOWANCES

	Age (yrs.)	Weight (lbs)	Height (in.)	Protein (grams)
Children	1–3	28	34	23
	4–6	44	44	30
	7–10	66	54	36
Males	11–14	97	63	44
	15–18	134	69	54
	19–22	147	69	54
	23–50	154	69	56
	51+	154	69	56
Female	11–14	97	62	44
	15–18	119	65	48
	19–22	128	65	46
	23–50	128	65	46
	51+	128	65	46
Pregnant				+30
Lactating				+20

APPENDIX 2

SUBSTITUTIONS AND EQUIVALENTS

1 cup butter	=	⅞ cup oil
1 cup butter	=	1 cup margarine
1 pound cottage cheese	=	2 cups
1 cup cottage cheese	=	1 cup mashed soft tofu
1 cup ricotta cheese	=	1 cup mashed soft tofu
4 ounces Cheddar cheese	=	1 cup grated
1 cup cream cheese	=	¾ cup mashed soft tofu plus ¼ cup soft butter plus 1 tablespoon lemon juice or vinegar
1 square unsweetened chocolate	=	3 tablespoons cocoa plus 1½ teaspoons oil
1 tablespoon cornstarch	=	2 tablespoons flour (for thickening)
1 egg white	=	2 teaspoons dried egg white plus 2 tablespoons warm water
1 egg yolk	=	2 tablespoons dried egg yolk plus 2 teaspoons water
1 whole egg	=	¼ cup soft tofu
1 whole egg	=	¼ cup soft tofu plus 2 teaspoons oil
1 whole egg	=	⅛ cup soft tofu plus a teaspoon dried egg white plus 2 tablespoons water
1 cup honey	=	1 cup molasses
1 cup sugar	=	⅞ cup honey plus ¼ teaspoon baking soda
1 cup cow's milk	=	1 cup soy milk
1 cup buttermilk	=	¾ cup soy milk plus 2 tablespoons vinegar or lemon juice plus 1 tablespoon soft butter

1 cup buttermilk	=	½ cup soft tofu plus ⅓ cup water or soy milk plus 2 tablespoons lemon juice or vinegar
1 cup sour cream	=	⅓ cup butter plus ½ cup soy milk plus 1 tablespoon lemon juice
1 cup sour cream	=	3 tablespoons oil or butter plus ⅔ cup soft tofu plus 1 tablespoon lemon juice
1 cup soft tofu, mashed	=	8 to 10 ounces soft tofu, by weight

APPENDIX 3

(Legend for columns on following page)

1. % Water
2. Calories or food energy
3. Protein (in grams)
4. Fat (in grams)
5. Cholesterol (in milligrams)
6. Carbohydrates (in grams)
7. Calcium (in milligrams)
8. Sodium (in milligrams)
9. Potassium (in milligrams)

NUTRIENTS IN SELECTED FOODS, 100 GRAMS (app. 3½ ounces)

100 gram portions about 3½ ounces	Wat. % 1	Cal 2	Pro (gm) 3	Fat (gm) 4	Chol. (mg) 5	CHO (gm) 6	Calc (mg) 7	Sod (mg) 8	Pot (mg) 9
Almonds, dried	4.7	598	18.6	54.2	0	19.5	234	4	773
Bananas	75.7	85	1.1	.2	0	22.2	8	1	370
Barley	10.8	348	9.6	1.1	0	77.2	34	0	296
Beans, white (cooked)	69.0	118	7.8	.6	0	21.2	50	7	416
Beef chuck (cooked)	49.4	327	26	23.9	70	0	11	60	370
Beef hamburger (raw 22% fat)	60.2	268	17.9	21.2	70	0	10	60	236
Bran (unprocessed)	see Wheat								
Bread, French	30.6	290	9.1	3	0	55.4	43	580	90
Bread, pumpernickel	34	246	9.1	1.2	0	53.1	84	569	454
Bread, white	35.6	270	8.7	3.2	0	50.5	84	507	105
Bread, whole-wheat	36.4	243	10.5	3	0	47.7	99	527	273
Butter, salted	15.5	716	.6	81	250	.4	20	987	23
Butter, unsalted	15.5	716	.6	81	250	.4	20	10	10
Buttermilk	90.5	36	3.6	.1	3	5.1	121	130	140
Carob powder	11.2	180	4.5	1.5	0	80.7	352	0	0

Cocoa powder	3	295	16.8	23.7	0	48.3	133	6	1,522
Cheese, Cheddar	37	398	25	32.2	100	2.1	750	700	82
Cheese, cream	51	374	8	37.7	120	2.1	62	250	74
Cheese, cottage (creamed)	78.3	106	13.6	4.2	15	2.9	94	229	85
Cheese, other (app. 25 to 30% fat)	30	370	27.5	28	85	1.7	925	710	104
Cheese, processed	40	370	23.2	30	100	1.9	697	1,136	80
Chicken, raw (without skin)	73.7	130	20.6	4.7	60	0	11	50	320
Cod, raw	81.2	78	17.6	.3	70		10	70	382
Corn, sweet, raw	72.7	96	3.5	1	0	22.1	3	t	280
Cornmeal	12	368	7.8	2.6	0	76.8	6	1	231
Crab, steamed	78.5	93	17.3	1.9	125	.5	43	0	0
Eggs, whole, fresh chicken	73.7	163	12.9	11.5	550	.9	54	122	129
Eggs, white, fresh	87.6	51	10.9	t	0	.8	9	146	139
Eggs, yolk, fresh	51.1	348	16	30.6	1,500	.6	141	52	98
Fish, raw (app.)	81	79	16	.8	70	0	12	78	342
Honey	17.2	304	.3	0	0	82.3	5	5	51
Lamb, raw, choice	60.8	262	16.9	21	70	0	10	75	295
Lentils, whole, dry	11.1	340	24.7	1.1	0	60.1	79	30	790
Macaroni, dry	10.4	369	12.5	1.2	0	75.2	27	2	197
Milk, whole	87.4	65	3.5	3.5	11	4.9	118	50	144

100 gram portions about 3½ ounces	Wat. % 1	Cal 2	Pro (gm) 3	Fat (gm) 4	Chol. (mg) 5	CHO (gm) 6	Calc (mg) 7	Sod (mg) 8	Pot (mg) 9
Milk, skimmed	90.5	36	3.6	.1	3	5.1	121	52	145
Millet	11.8	327	9.9	2.9	0	72.9	20	0	430
Oats, rolled, dry	8.3	390	14.2	7.4	0	68.2	53	2	352
Oysters, raw	84.6	66	8.4	1.8	200	3.4	94	73	121
Pasta, dry (without egg)	10.4	383	12.9	4.1	0	71.8	35	5	195
Peanuts, roasted, unsalted	1.8	582	26.2	48.7	0	20.6	72	5	701
Peas, dry, split	9.3	348	24.2	1	0	62.7	33	40	895
Pork, raw, lean	69.3	171	17.8	10.5	70	0	10	70	285
Pork, cooked ham	53.6	289	20.9	22.1	70	0	9	930	326
Pork, fried bacon	8.1	611	30.4	52	70	3.2	14	1,021	236
Potatoes, baked	75.1	93	2.6	.1	0	21.1	9	4	503
Potatoes, peeled, boiled	82.8	65	1.9	.1	0	14.5	6	2	285
Rice, brown, raw	12	360	7.5	1.9	0	77.4	32	9	214
Rice, white, raw	12	363	6.7	.4	0	80.4	24	5	92
Rice bran	9.7	276	13.3	15.8	0	50.8	76	t	1,495
Rye, whole grain	11	334	12.1	1.7	0	73.4	38	1	467
Rye, flour	11	327	16.3	2.6	0	68.1	54	1	860

Salmon, raw	64.2	222	19.1	15.6	70	0	0	45	399
Sesame seeds, dry	5.8	582	17.2	52.8	0	19.8	750	49	508
Sesame paste (tahini)	.2	600	19.2	52.3	0	23.5	960	0	582
Shrimp, raw	78.2	91	18.1	.8	125	1.5	63	140	220
Soybeans, dry, uncooked	10	403	34.1	17.7	0	33.5	226	5	1,677
Soybean-curd, soft Tofu	84.8	72	7.8	4.2	0	2.4	128	7	42
Soybean curd, firm Tofu	76	113	13.3	6.5	0	3.1	136	6	154
Soybean curd, dry PSP	6.8	461	47	28.4	0	14.9	245	124	463
Soy flour, full-fat	8	421	36.7	20.3	0	30.4	199	1	1,660
Soy flour, defatted	8	326	47	.9	0	38.1	265	1	1,820
Soy milk	91.4	37	2.8	1.5	0	3.6	18	15	58
Soy residue, Okara	83.9	67	3.4	1.5	0	10.4	86	0	95
Soy sauce	62.8	68	5.6	1.3	0	9.5	82	7,325	366
Spaghetti, dry	10.4	369	12.5	1.2	0	75.2	27	2	197
Sugar, cane or beet, all kinds	.5	385	0	0	0	99.5	0	1	3
Sunflower seeds, dry	4.8	560	24	47.3	0	19.9	120	30	920
Tofu (see soy)									
Tuna, canned, oil packed, drained	60.6	197	28.8	8.2	70	0	8	41	301

100 gram portions / about 3½ ounces	Wat. % 1	Cal 2	Pro (gm) 3	Fat (gm) 4	Chol. (mg) 5	CHO (gm) 6	Calc (mg) 7	Sod (mg) 8	Pot (mg) 9
Tuna, water pack	70	127	28	.8	70	0	16	41	279
Turkey, without skin, cooked	61.2	190	31.5	6.1	60	0	8	130	367
Veal, raw	66	207	18.8	14	90	0	11	90	320
Walnuts, English	3.5	651	14.8	64	0	15.8	99	2	450
Wheat, whole-grain	14	326	10.2	2	0	72.1	42	3	376
Wheat flour, whole	12	333	13.3	2	0	71	41	3	370
Wheat, enriched, all-purpose bleached	12	364	10.5	1	0	76.1	16	2	95
Wheat bran	11.5	213	16	4.6	0	61.9	119	9	1,121
Wheat germ	11.5	363	26.6	10.9	0	46.7	72	3	827
Yeast, baker's dry	5	282	36.9	1.6	0	38.9	44	52	1,998
Yeast, Brewer's	5	283	38.8	1	0	38.4	210	121	1,894
Yeast, torula	6	277	38.6	1	0	37	424	15	2,046
Yogurt, whole	88	62	3	3.4	11	4.9	111	47	132
Yogurt, low fat	89	50	3.4	1.7	6	5.2	120	51	143

Source of information:

Composition of Foods, Agriculture Handbook No. 8, Agricultural Research Service, U.S. Department of Agriculture, Washington, D.C., Revised 1963, Reprinted, 1975.

Food Composition Table for use in East Asia, U.S. Department of Health, Education and Welfare, 1972.

INDEX

ABOUT THE AUTHOR

Tofu is a way of life for JUEL ANDERSEN. Since becoming interested in this favorite Oriental food she has spent much time developing ways to use tofu in American cooking. She is the author of TOFU PRIMER and co-author of THE TOFU COOKBOOK. Ms. Andersen lives in Northern California with her family (and dog, Tofu) where she teaches tofu cooking at several colleges.

SLIM DOWN!
STAY HEALTHY!

These bestselling Bantam books can help

THE BEVERLY HILLS MEDICAL DIET
by Arnold Fox, M.D.
The bestselling rapid weight-loss diet that's sweeping the country. Lose 10 pounds in 14 days without stress. You can enjoy potatoes, pasta and other "forbidden foods" from Dr. Fox's extraordinary thin cuisine. THE BEVERLY HILLS MEDICAL DIET includes hundreds of scrumptious all-natural recipes and a lifetime Maintenance Plan to stay permanently healthy and slim. (#20528-5 • $2.75)

DIET FOR LIFE
by Francine Prince
You can lose 8 pounds in 14 days with bestselling author Francine Prince's quick and easy-to-follow plan for weight loss and a healthier, more invigorating life. This time-tested program will help you win the fight against nutrition-related diseases such as heart attack, hypertension, and diabetes without drugs and will help you to reduce to your ideal weight—and stay there—while savoring over 100 nutritious and high-energy recipes. (#20484-X • $3.50)

How's Your Health?

Bantam publishes a line of informative books, written by top experts to help you toward a healthier and happier life.

☐ 20475 **DR. ATKINS' SUPERENERGY DIET,** $3.50
   Robert Atkins, M.D.

☐ 20065 **FASTING: The Ultimate Diet,** Allan Cott, M.D. $2.50

☐ 20322 **HEALTH FOR THE WHOLE PERSON:** $3.95
   The Complete Guide to Holistic Health
   Hastings, et. al.

☐ 14075 **THE COMPLETE SCARSDALE MEDICAL DIET** $3.50
   Tarnower & Baker

☐ 20175 **A DICTIONARY OF SYMPTOMS,** J. Gomez $3.95

☐ 14221 **THE BRAND NAME NUTRITION COUNTER,** $2.50
   Jean Carper

☐ 13629 **SWEET AND DANGEROUS,** John Yudkin, M.D. $2.50

☐ 20086 **NUTRITION AGAINST DISEASE,** $2.95
   Roger J. Williams

☐ 01299 **MY BODY MY HEALTH** $9.95
   Stewarts, Hatcher, Guest

☐ 14561 **NUTRITION AND YOUR MIND,** George Watson $2.75

☐ 20409 **HOW TO LIVE 365 DAYS A YEAR** $2.95
   THE SALT FREE WAY,
   Brunswick, Love & Weinberg

☐ 20621 **THE PILL BOOK** Simon & Silverman $3.95

☐ 20134 **PRITIKIN PROGRAM FOR DIET AND** $3.95
   EXERCISE, Pritikin & McGrady, Jr.

☐ 13977 **THE ALL-IN-ONE CARBOHYDRATE GRAM** $2.50
   COUNTER, Jean Carper

☐ 20130 **WHICH VITAMINS DO YOU NEED?** $2.75
   Martin Ebon

☐ 20856 **FASTING AS A WAY OF LIFE,** Allan Cott, M.D. $2.50

☐ 20339 **THE ALL-IN-ONE CALORIE COUNTER,** $2.95
   Jean Carper

☐ 13259 **THE FAMILY GUIDE TO BETTER FOOD AND** $2.50
   BETTER HEALTH, Ron Deutsch

☐ 20530 **PSYCHODIETETICS,** Cheraskin, et al. $2.75

Buy them at your local bookstore or use this handy coupon for ordering: